Beside Still Waters
A Journey of Comfort and Renewal

עַל מֵי מְנוּחוֹת

Published by Ben Yehuda Press
122 Ayers Court #1B
Teaneck, NJ 07666
http://www.BenYehudaPress.com
ISBN13 978-1-934730-01-0

19 20 21 / 6 5 4 3   20190305

Dedicated to the memory of
Eleanor Meyerhoff Katz.

Contents

Dedication

Rabbi Dr. Shohama Harris Wiener

Beside Still Waters seeks presence and wholeness in the shadow of absence and loss. Amidst a loved one's illness and death, the eminently human journey of caring, losing, grieving, yearning, confounding, rising and renewing often asks all that we are – and sometimes more than we feel we can be.

Shohama Harris Wiener has been our teacher and mentor in these ways of spirit. Shohama's decades of service blazed trails in spirituality and clergy formation, attuning hundreds of spiritual leaders and seekers to the life of the soul.

As President of the Academy for Jewish Religion, Shohama was history's first woman to lead a Jewish seminary, infusing tradition with deep spiritual wisdom. As the first Rosh Hashpa'ah (Head of Spiritual Direction) and Founding Director of the Hashpa'ah training program at ALEPH, Shohama wove a tapestry of spirituality and clergy training unique in modern Jewish life. As rabbi of Temple Beth El of City Island (New York, NY), Shohama has modeled authenticity of spirit and awakened countless others to the possibility of joyfully spiritual Judaism in their own lives. As wife, mother, grandmother, mentor and friend, Shohama's gently empowering ways have nourished both her own family and a soul family that spans the globe.

Because Shohama's presence resonates so deeply in our lives and our rabbinates, we lovingly dedicate this volume to Shohama. We are grateful beyond measure for all that Shohama continues to teach, the Waters of Healing that are her life's wellspring, and the expanding circle of students who serve as her legacy.

Marianne Williamson's words about spirit aptly describe Shohama's life: "As we let our own light shine, we unconsciously give other people permission to do the same. As we are liberated from our own fear, our presence automatically liberates others."

In the merit of our teacher, so may it be for all whom this volume supports on the soul's journey of love, loss and healing.

Rachel, Evan, David and Jennifer

Introduction

Stages on the Journey

Death is part of life. While we live, the deaths of others bring us loss and grief, sometimes relief and sometimes ambivalence. When our own lives end, we transition into something that we cannot know. This book is intended to help navigate the continuum of living, in health and illness, healing or dying, and the transitions that come after a death for those who remain.

If a death is not sudden, if illness offers "advance warning" or opportunity to prepare, both the person who is dying and the person who is preparing to mark that death as a mourner are likely to experience deep emotions and ask big questions.

The sections of this volume entitled "Healing of Body," "Healing of Spirit," and "Before Death" contain readings and prayers for this time. These readings and prayers may be helpful for the person who is sick and for the person who anticipates marking a loss yet to come.

The next stage comes after a person has died, but before burial. One Jewish tradition holds that the soul of the person who has died lingers near their body until burial, which is the reason that some maintain the custom of *sh'mira*, keeping watch over the body and keeping company with the soul of the deceased. For the mourner, this stage is called *aninut*. The period between death and interment can be a tender space and one of emotionally unstable days. The section of this volume entitled "Before Burial" contains readings and prayers for this time.

After the burial, the mourner enters the first week after burial, known as *shiva* ("seven"). At this time, the Hebrew term for such a mourner is *avel* or *avela*, and this period is also known as *avelut*. During this first week, it's customary for the community to gather in the mourner's home to keep them company, to care for them, and to constitute a *minyan* (a quorum of ten adult Jews) so that the mourner can recite prayers of mourning in the loving presence of community. More on that at the beginning of the "*Shiva*" chapter.

When a Holiday Cancels *Shiva*

When a Jewish holiday arrives during *shiva*, the *shiva* is cut short. Rosh Hashanah, Yom Kippur, the first day of Sukkot or Passover or Shavuot: all of these curtail *shiva*. This is true even if the festival begins on the evening of the day of the funeral. In these cases, the regular rhythms of grieving are disrupted, which can be emotionally and spiritually challenging. There are prayers for that circumstance in the After *Shiva* chapter of this book.

Following *shiva*, the mourner is in the period called *sh'loshim* ("thirty"), the first month after burial. That first month is followed by the following months that round out the year until the first *yahrzeit* (death-anniversary). In the classical Jewish tradition, one mourns a parent for a year (or, some say: for eleven months — presuming that saying Kaddish helps to purify and elevate the soul of the deceased, and only a *rasha*, a wicked person, would require twelve months of that uplifting) and one mourns other intimate family members for one month. In today's world, many of us mourn many relationships (not only parents) for a full eleven or twelve months.

In addition to the *yahrzeit* or death-anniversary, Jewish tradition offers four opportunities each year for communal remembering, at the four Yizkor (Remembrance / Memorial) services of the festival year. In this volume, the sections entitled "After *Shiva*," "*Yahrzeit*," and "*Yizkor*" contain readings for those seasons, while the chapter entitled "Remembrance" offers prayers and poems of remembrance that can be used at any time.

The paradigm in which mourning unfolds through these distinct stages offers one truth: the first days after a death are likely to feel different from the first week, which, in turn, is different from the first month, the first year and so on. Another truth is that grief is rarely linear: It unfolds in its own time. Grief has an ebb and flow (in the language of tradition, a *ratzo vashov*, "running and returning"). Many who experience grief find that they can't control those tides, but rather just ride them. Your experience will be uniquely yours.

Our hope is that this volume will help those who are on the mourner's path... with awareness that all of us eventually experience this path, in many different ways over the course of our lives.

How to Use This Book

This book offers readings, prayers, reflections, and practices: beginning before death, with prayers for healing and prayers to recite before dying, and continuing through the first *yahrzeit* and subsequent *Yizkor* memorials.

If you are part of a community that will accompany you in sitting *shiva*, the *shiva* liturgies in this book will give you prayers (whether you choose an afternoon observance or an evening one) for *shiva minyanim* / services.

If you are not part of a community, or are mourning on your own, you can still use this book and the liturgies it contains. Although certain prayers (including the Bar'chu call to prayer and the Kaddish in all of its forms) are traditionally only recited in the presence of a *minyan*, even a solitary mourner may find comfort in the traditional words and forms — or in the creative, interpretive, renewed / renewing variations that appear alongside the classical tradition.

On Language

Hebrew and English

For millennia, Hebrew has been Judaism's holy language of prayer. For those who are comfotable with Hebrew, its poetry and its resonance can be profound. And for those who are not fluent in Hebrew, the rhythms and sounds of the traditional prayers (especially the Mourner's Kaddish) can be evocative and meaningful in ways that go beyond literal linguistic comprehension. For this reason, we provide the liturgy of *shiva* and the memorial prayers of Yizkor here in Hebrew.

All of the Hebrew in this book is also transliterated and translated into English. Vernacular prayer can be powerful, and can provide comfort, especially at times of mourning. Reb Zalman z"l (Rabbi Zalman Schachter-Shalomi, of blessed memory — one of the *zaides*/grandfathers of Jewish renewal) taught that prayer needs to come from the heart, and sometimes that means that the pray-er (the person who is praying) needs to be speaking their own familiar language.

Translation

Every translation is a choice, and Hebrew is a rich and multi-layered language. Even a simple and familiar phrase, such as

בָּרוּךְ אַתָּה, יהוה אֱלֹהֵינוּ, מֶלֶךְ הָעוֹלָם...
Baruch atah, יהוה Eloheinu, Melech haolam...

can be rendered in English in a variety of ways. Here are three equally faithful translations:

Blessed are You, Lord our God, King of the universe...
A Fountain of Blessings are You, יהוה our God, Sovereign of all worlds...
You are blessed, Infinite Is/Was/Will-Be, our God, Core of all that is...

We've chosen one way of rendering these words throughout this book, but if a different one resonates more for you, feel free to substitute it, either aloud or in your head and heart.

Reb Zalman z"l also compared printed liturgy to freeze-dried soup: the ingredients are there, but in order for the soup to be nourishing, one must add hot water. In any printed liturgy, the ingredients are there, but, in order for the prayer to be nourishing, the pray-er must add intention and heart. May this volume give you the resources you need in order to offer the prayers of your heart as you walk the mourner's path.

Ways of Speaking to the One

God has many names in Jewish tradition, among them *Elohim* (God), יהוה (or *YHVH*: an untranslatable permutation of the verb "to be"), *Havayah* (like יהוה, a permutation of the verb "to be"), *Ahavah* (Love), *Adonai* (Lord), *Shechinah* (immanent, indwelling, feminine Presence), *Ein haChayyim* (Source of Life) *Melech* (King), *Malkah* (Queen), *Ruach* (Breath of Life), *Avinu* (Our Father), *Immeinu* (Our Mother), Beloved, Friend, Creator, Wellspring, Source, Hidden One, Merciful One, Judge, Parent, and many more.

Most of our traditional prayers use masculine God-language (Lord, Father, King), like so:

בָּרוּךְ אַתָּה, יהוה אֱלֹהֵינוּ, מֶלֶךְ הָעוֹלָם...

Baruch atah, יהוה Eloheinu, Melech haolam...

Blessed are You, יהוה our God, Sovereign of the Universe...

Today, some find that feminine language (Queen, Mother, *Shechinah*) enables them to better speak to the One. That might mean using feminine names for God(dess), and it might mean feminizing the Hebrew, like so:

בְּרוּכָה אַתְּ, יָה שְׁכִינָה, רוּחַ הָעוֹלָם...

B'ruchah at, Yah Sh'chinah, Ruach haolam...

Blessed are You, Shechinah, Breath of the World...

Although most of the liturgy in this book follows the traditional masculine paradigm, in some places a feminine alternative is also offered (for instance, *El Malei Rachamim* is accompanied by *Elah M'lei'at Rachamim*: that same prayer invoking Divine compassion, but spoken to a divinity that is gendered female, rather than a divinity that is gendered male.)

Still others prefer gender-neutral terms (Friend, Source, Wellspring), such as:

נְבָרֵךְ אֶת עֵין הַחַיִּים...

N'vareich et Ein hachayyim...

Let us bless the Source of Life...

Use whatever words best enable you to relate to the Divine.

Jewish tradition teaches that our Creator is beyond language: our words can only approach the Infinite. May our linguistic choices remind us that our names are only substitutes, and that our Source is beyond any words we can speak.

Healing of Body, Healing of Spirit

Healing is not the same as cure. A cure may not always be possible, but we can always pray for greater healing of body, heart, mind, and spirit. Sometimes the heart and spirit can be healed even when the body cannot.

Prayers for Healing

Mi Shebeirach / Prayer for Healing

מִי שֶׁבֵּרַךְ אֲבוֹתֵינוּ,	Mi shebeirach avoteinu,
אַבְרָהָם, יִצְחָק, וְיַעֲקֹב,	Avraham, Yitzchak, v'Ya·akov,
וְאִמוֹתֵינוּ,	v'imoteinu,
שָׂרָה, רִבְקָה, רָחֵל, וְלֵאָה,	Sarah, Rivkah, Racheil, v'Lei·ah,
הוּא יְבָרֵךְ אֶת חוֹלֵי הַנֶּפֶשׁ,	Hu y'vareich et cholei hanefesh,
חוֹלֵי הָרוּחַ וְחוֹלֵי הַגּוּף.	cholei haruach, v'cholei haguf.
הַקָּדוֹשׁ בָּרוּךְ הוּא יִהְיֶה עִמָּהֶם	haKadosh, baruch Hu, yihyeh imahem
וּשְׁמָר לָהֶם.	ushmar lahem.
חַזֵּק אֶת יָדָם בְּאֹמֶץ־לֵב	Chazeik et yadam b'ometz-lev
בְּכָל יוֹם,	b'chol yom,
בְּתוֹךְ שְׁאָר כָּל הַחוֹלִים	b'toch sh'ar kol hacholim
הַשְׁתָּא בַּעֲגָלָא וּבִזְמַן קָרִיב,	hashta ba·agala uvizman kariv;
וְנֹאמַה אָמֵן.	v'nomar: Amen.

May the One who blessed our ancestors,
Abraham, Isaac and Jacob,
Sarah, Rebecca, Rachel and Leah,
bless those in need of healing of body, mind and spirit.
May the compassion of the Holy One be upon them
and watch over them.
Strengthen them with courage in each day,
along with all who are ill,
now and swiftly.
And let us say: Amen.

Waters of Healing

May the waters of healing flow through our soul.
May the waters of healing flow through our mind.
May the waters of healing flow through our heart.
May the waters of healing flow through our form.

Ana el na, please Holy One,
Refa na lah, let Your healing be done.
Ana el na, heal our soul,
Refa na lah, may we be whole.

May the pure light of healing flow through our soul.
May the pure light of healing flow through our mind.
May the pure light of healing flow through our heart.
May the pure light of healing flow through our form.

(Rabbi Shohama Wiener)

Help Us to See Illness

Dear God, help us to see illness
not as our enemy
but as an inevitable element
of life in these vessels.
Help us celebrate our lives in these bodies.

Let us all be Psalmists
singing Your praise with every breath,
and with every ache and pain too,
for as long as we can, and
may it be long, and may it end gently.

Dear God, that's at the heart of what we want.
Death scares us and we can't see beyond it.
We want to live.
We want to live a long time.
And then we want it to end gently.

Sometimes we might be willing
to suffer in order to be here longer.
And sometimes we might be willing
to let go a little earlier
if suffering is the price of life.

If it's possible,
let us make those decisions,
each of us for ourselves.

Heal us, God.
And if healing of the body is out of reach,
Then may we open to You like a riverbed,
and may Your peace pour in like water.

(Irwin Keller)

Before Death

Prayers Before Death

Before death, it is customary to recite a confessional prayer called a *vidui*.

This name is also given to the confessional prayer recited on Yom Kippur. Some Jews have a custom of reciting a *vidui* before bed each night in order to cultivate *t'shuvah* (repentance / return) and forgiveness before sleep. Others have a custom of reciting a *vidui* on weekdays as part of daily prayer.

Because a *vidui* can be recited daily, there is nothing "wrong" with praying a *vidui* when one is not dying. There is also no need to have a rabbi or clergyperson present. This is not like the Catholic tradition of the Sacrament of the Sick (formerly known as Last Rites), which should be said only on one's deathbed with a priest present.

Although many of the confessional prayers included in this volume are intended to be recited by someone who is dying, it's okay to pray them even if one doesn't die immediately thereafter. It's okay to pray them more than once, as needed.

And, if someone has died and you don't know whether or not they said a *vidui* prayer on their deathbed, some Jews have the custom of reciting a *vidui* on behalf of the deceased at the funeral before placing earth atop the casket.

Vidui: Deathbed Prayer for Release

אֱלֹהַי וֵאלֹהֵי אֲבוֹתַי וְאִמּוֹתַי,
שְׁמַע בְּקוֹלִי.

men say: מוֹדֶה women say: מוֹדָה
אֲנִי לְפָנֶיךָ, מְקוֹר הַבְּרָכָה,
שֶׁנִּשְׁמָתִי וְגוּפִי מְסוּרִים בְּיָדֶךָ.
אֱלֹהַי, נְשָׁמָה שֶׁנָּתַתָּ בִּי טְהוֹרָה
הִיא: אַתָּה בְרָאתָהּ,
אַתָּה יְצַרְתָּהּ, אַתָּה נְפַחְתָּהּ בִּי,
וְאַתָּה מְשַׁמְּרָהּ בְּקִרְבִּי עַד
הַיּוֹם הַזֶּה. יְהִי רָצוֹן מִלְּפָנֶיךָ, אַב
הָרַחֲמָן, שֶׁתִּרְפָּאֵנִי רְפוּאָה שְׁלֵמָה.
וּכְשֶׁאֶעֱבֹר מֵעוֹלָם הַזֶּה,
אִם הַיּוֹם אוֹ בִּזְמַן עָתִיד לָבוֹא,
תְּחָנֵּנִי וְקֵרוּבֵי הַלְּבִי, שֶׁמִּתְחַבְּרִים
עִם נִשְׁמָתִי, לְהַסְכִּים אֶת פְּנִיַּת שֶׁל
גַּלְגַּל הַחַיִּים הַזֹּאת.
לְפָנֶיךָ אֵל רַחוּם וְחַנּוּן, מְכַפֵּר עָוֹן
וְלֹא מַשְׁחִית, אֲנִי

men say: סוֹלֵחַ women say: סוֹלַחַת
כָּל שֶׁהֵרְעוּנִי בְּחַיַּי. תִּהְיוּ רְגוּעוֹת
לְבוֹתֵיהֶם וַאֲשַׁלֵּחַ מִמֶּנִּי
כָּל כַּעַס וּכְאָב מֵהֶם לְתוֹךְ אֵפֶר
הָאָרֶץ. כְּשֵׁם שֶׁסָּלַחְתִּי לַאֲחֵרִים,
כֵּן תִּסְלַח לִי מִכָּל הַחֲטָאִים שֶׁלִּי.
בִּזְכוּת זֶה, תִּשְׁמוֹר אֶת נִשְׁמָתִי
בְּשָׁלוֹם וּתְזְהַר נַפְשִׁי כְּזוֹהַר הָרָקִיעַ
לְעוֹלָמִים.
אֲנִי

women say מַאֲמִינָה men say מַאֲמִין
בְּאֱמוּנָה שְׁלֵמָה שֶׁתְּקַבֵּל
נִשְׁמָתִי בְּאַהֲבָה.
גַּם כִּי אֵלֵךְ בְּגֵיא צַלְמָוֶת
לֹא אִירָא רָע כִּי אַתָּה עִמָּדִי.
בְּיָדְךָ אַפְקִיד רוּחִי פָּדִיתָה אוֹתִי
יהוה אֵל אֱמֶת.
שְׁמַע יִשְׂרָאֵל, יהוה אֱלֹהֵינוּ,
יהוה אֶחָד.
יהוה הָאֱלֹהִים. יהוה הָאֱלֹהִים.
יהוה הָאֱלֹהִים.

Elohai, veilohei avotai v'imotai,
sh'ma b'koli.

men say: Modeh   women say: Modah
ani l'fanecha, M'kor haB'racha,
shenishmati v'gufi m'surim b'yadecha.
Elohai, n'shamah shenatata bi
t'horah hi: Atah v'ratah,
atah y'tzartah, atah n'fachtah bi,
v'atah m'sham'rah b'kirbi ad
hayom hazeh. Y'hi ratzon mil'fanecha, Av
Harachaman, shet'rap'eini r'fuah sh'leimah.
Uchshe·e·evor mei·olam hazzeh,
im hayom o bazman atid lavo,
t'chaneini v'kruvei halibi shemit·chab'rim
im nishmati l'haskim et p'niyyat shel
galgal hachayyim hazot.
L'fanecha El rachum v'chanun, m'chapeir avon
v'lo mash·chit, ani

men say: solei·ach   women say: solachat
kol sheheirei·uni b'chayai. Tiyu r'gu·ot
liboteihem va'ashallei·ach mimeni
kol kaas uch'eiv meiheim l'toch eifer
ha·aretz. K'sheim shesalachti l'acheirim,
kein tislach li mikol hachata·im shelli.
Bizchut zeh, tishmor et nishmati
b'shalom utiz·har nafshi k'zohar haraki·a
l'olamim.
Ani

men say ma·amin women say ma·aminah
be·emunah sh'leimah shet'kabel
nishmati b'ahavah.
Gam ki eilech b'gei tzalmavet
lo ira ra ki atah imadi.
B'yad'cha afkid ruchi padita oti
יהוה El emet.
Sh'ma Yisra·el, יהוה Eloheinu,
יהוה Echad.
יהוה ha·Elohim. יהוה ha·Elohim.
יהוה ha·Elohim.

Vidui: Deathbed Prayer for Release

My God and God of my ancestors, hear my voice.

I acknowledge before You, Source of Blessing, that my soul and body are in Your hands. My God, the soul You gave me is pure: You created it, formed it, breathed it into me and kept it safe in me until now. May it be Your will, Source of Compassion, that You grant me complete healing. But when I pass from this world – whether today or in a time to come – grant me and the beloveds of my heart, whose souls are bound with mine, the grace to accept this turning of the wheel of life.

Before You, God of Mercy and Grace who pardons iniquity and does not destroy, I forgive all who harmed me in my life. May their hearts be at ease, as I release all anger and pain from them into the dust of the earth. As I have forgiven, so may You forgive me all my shortcomings. By this merit, preserve my soul in peace; may my spirit forever shine as the brightness of the firmament.

I believe with perfect faith that You will accept my soul in love. Even when I walk through the valley of the shadow of death, I will fear no evil for You are with me.

Into Your hand I surrender my spirit: You redeem me, God of Truth.
Hear, O Israel, יהוה is our God, יהוה is One.
יהוה is the Eternal God. יהוה is the Eternal God. יהוה is the Eternal God.

(Rabbi David Evan Markus)

Short *Vidui*

I acknowledge before the Source of All
that life and death are not in my hands.

Just as my soul chose to enter this world in life,
so my soul chooses to depart this world in death.

May my life be a healing memory
for those who knew me.

May my loved ones think well of me,
and may my memory bring them joy.

From all those I may have hurt, I ask forgiveness.
To all who have hurt me, I grant forgiveness.

As a wave returns to the ocean,
so I return to the Source from which I came.

שְׁמַע, יִשְׂרָאֵל, יהוה אֱלֹהֵינוּ, יהוה אֶחָד.
Sh'ma, Yisra·eil: יהוה Eloheinu, יהוה Echad!
Hear, O Israel: יהוה is our God; יהוה is One.

(Rabbi Rachel Barenblat)

Vidui for Mourners of Painful Relationships

My God and God of the generations of my people, I am distressed and confused. Hear my prayer; answer me with compassion.

During my lifetime I have experienced misunderstanding, hurt, and harm in my relationship with _____.

Though I have sought help and understanding, I have not found peace nor recovered from painful experience and memories. I have been unable to forgive _____, neither have I found the ways to forgive myself for my own confusion, anger, and suffering.

Some days I feel no hope for connection and reconciliation. This is a painful passage; I have no answers, but my questions cry out:

How can I approach this period of mourning? How shall I mark this death? How can I fulfill my obligation as a _____ to one who has been a source of my grief? How can I find solace in my community if I feel different from other mourners? Without a community, where will I find my help? With whom can I share this particular pain? How can I be most true to myself, for my own sake? What do I need at this time?

From a place of narrowness I cry out; please free me! Breathe into me the breath of healing spaciousness.

(Alison Jordan)

Vidui: For All the Ways

Inevitably, all lives
rub up against other lives
and so has mine
for good and for harm.

For all the ways
my life has touched others
in love, in compassion,
in wisdom, in justice,
in joy, in wonder,
in healing, in grace,
in ordinary kindness,
knowing or unknowing,
I am grateful.

For all the ways
other lives have touched mine
in love, in compassion,
in wisdom, in justice,
in joy, in wonder,
in healing, in grace,
in ordinary kindness,
knowing or unknowing,
I am grateful.

For all the ways
my life has touched others
in anger, in cruelty,
in hurtfulness, in unfairness,
in ignorance, in numbness,
in narrowness, in selfishness,
in carelessness, in unmindfulness,
knowing or unknowing,
I ask forgiveness,
to the extent that it is possible.

For all the ways
the lives of others have touched mine
in anger, in cruelty,
in hurtfulness, in unfairness
in ignorance, in numbness,
in narrowness, in selfishness,
in carelessness, in unmindfulness,
knowing or unknowing,
I offer forgiveness,
to the extent that I am able.

And to all the mysteries,
all that remains uncertain and unknown,
all that I do not know about reasons or outcomes,
all that I do not know about right or wrong
or harm or healing,
I offer my surrender.

My intention is that the sum total of my life
be for the good.
Yehi ratzon milifnei Shekhinah:
May this, may all this, be acceptable
before the Presence.

I ask this in all the worlds,
from all the worlds,
in this time
and for all time:
Le'olam ul'almei almaya.
Amen.

(Rabbi Jill Hammer)

Vidui Before Sleep

This prayer comes from the liturgy of the bedtime Sh'ma, and is designed to be recited each night before sleep. It can also be used as a vidui *at the end of life.*

You, My Eternal Friend,
Witness that I forgive anyone
who hurt or upset me or offended me -
damaging my body, my property,
my reputation or people that I love;
whether by accident or willfully,
carelessly or purposely,
with words, deeds, thought, or attitudes;
in this lifetime or another incarnation -
I forgive every person,
May no one be punished because of me.
Help me, Eternal Friend,
to keep from offending You and others.
Help me to be thoughtful
and not commit outrage,
by doing what is evil in Your eyes.
Whatever sins I have committed,
blot out please, in Your abundant kindness
and spare me suffering or harmful illnesses.
Hear the words of my mouth and
may the meditations of my heart
find acceptance before You, Eternal Friend,
Who protects and frees me. Amen.

(Translated by Rabbi Zalman Schachter-Shalomi z"l)

Before Burial

Between Death and Burial

The time after someone has died and before they are buried is called *aninut*. It can feel like a strange kind of limbo for mourners: the death has taken place, but the customs and rituals of *shiva* have not yet begun.

Here are prayers and poems to read during that tender time.

Gone

You're gone.
I don't know where you are.
Who am I without you?

(Rabbi David Evan Markus)

Aninut

The stalks were easy to snap
just above the root, brittle already
from flirting with first frost.
Still, they held clusters
of tiny gold flowers

until I broke them free and
laced each stem across the top
of our sukkah, merest hint
of roof holding back
the darkening sky.

By morning they blossomed
anew, each tight bud
now a puffball of white fur
spiced with seeds. In a week
we'll fling the remnants

past the forest's edge,
let these old husks fade.
Come spring they'll sprout
somewhere, maybe here, though
I doubt they'll remember

these days suspended in the sun,
air crisp like apples and sweet
with new-mown grass, bees
carrying the memory of summer
back to their hidden hives.

(Rabbi Rachel Barenblat)
For Sandy Ryan, after the death of her father.

The Tearing

Karov Adonai l'nishb'rei lev.
God is close to the brokenhearted.

(Psalm 34)

There is nothing so whole as a broken heart.

(The Kotzker Rebbe)

Nothing can be sole or whole/That has not been rent.

(WB Yeats)

Rend your covering
from top to bottom —
the curtain of your Temple.

The world is replete with loss, ordered by chaos.
Viewed through water-filled eyes
One thing is clear:
Garments are flimsy shields, thin veneers, temporary veils.

To rend is to expose,
To make visible the broken heart beating beneath,
To make audible the violent separation of what has been so painstakingly woven,
Torn ragged by hands just strong enough to do what they must,
The warp and weft at once sundered.

Unevenly.

(Rabbi Janet Madden)

A Prayer During Aninut

I'm alone and afraid.
Not knowing how to live with my loss.
Not understanding where my loved one has gone.
Everywhere I turn, more questions and wonderings.
Ruminating: From where will I draw strength?

Praised are You, Holy One of Blessing, Ruler of the Universe,
    Who accompanies me in this space between life and death.
Envelop me in Your wings; show me how to live in the chasm.
At this time of mystery, teach me to breathe through my pain.
Carry me toward comfort and connect me to the soul of my beloved.
Enfold me in Your light and hold me in Your love.

Amen.

(Rabbi Amy Grossblatt Pessah)

For One Who Did Not Want Ritual Mourning

How do I mark a loss that leaves no ritual trace? You imagined for yourself no mourners crowded together over the earth becoming your body, no weeping against the rising murmur of grief that holds everyone, no rending of cloth, no resisting and difficult assent to God's perfect judgment. My body struggles to keep from standing up into your memory, my tongue to keep from blessing your name in those strange syllables. In no moment and in every moment, the rising and weeping and struggling move nonetheless through my veins, fever dreams my spirit cannot forget.

(Jacqui Shine)

How Dying Works

It takes different
degrees of time
for each soul
to ripen.

When it is ready
to drop from one
dimension into another,
the sac of matter
dies away from it
to release it.

Spinning or
throwing forth or
flowing or sliding
away, the sac returns
to earth, air, fire
and water, and when
Earth herself dies
everything here
will go back
into stars.

Meanwhile, the individual
soul being born into
a new form becomes
a kind of supernova
star, gigantic, beautiful,
devastatingly bright,
hot with Godfire
as it explodes into
Everywhere.

Other souls who vibrate
to this light's same music
through love or likeness
become opened, and by

magnetic resonance and
attraction, shards
of the dying person's
soulfire pierce the souls
of others.

So we say our hearts
are broken and we do not
know ourselves for a time,
while we incorporate these
piercings of the beloved.

This is why it hurts
and this is how we become
opened and larger and lighter
ourselves, for we carry
these shards within us
Forever.

The more we lose,
the more open, large and
bright we become.

When we explode
into the Infinite
we are more than ourselves
already. We are many.
We are all who have become
a part of us in love
and all who will become.
It is all true.

Heaven is not a there.
Heaven is not somewhere.
Heaven is now, here,
streaming through.

(Alla Renée Bozarth)

To A Friend Who Has Departed

The following words to a departed soul may be of use to a mourner who needs to work through fears about the unknown, and may be of use to a departed soul that lingers and is listening.

My friend, dear＿＿＿＿＿, listen now, for that which is called death has come and gone. You have experienced the process of dissolving out of your body. The edges of who you were have become less defined. The sensations of your body are no longer so distinct, leaving just a spaciousness. Do not be afraid. יהוה will protect you from all disturbing thoughts and guard your soul. יהוה will guard your exit and entry from this world to the next. This transition you are going through need not be difficult or distressing. It is a natural part of existence which everyone ever born has to someday negotiate. This is your time to do so. Keep letting go gently, gently, of all that holds you back. You have already traversed what is called death. It is over. Open to it. Let go into it.

You may be experiencing the changing nature of the mind as it separates more and more from the body. Part of your task now is to dissolve into the stream of pure light. Let go gently, gently, without the least force. My dear friend, the dear light of your original nature is more revealed now that you have undergone this great release from your heavier form. Before you shines your true being. Approach it with reverence and compassion. You have seen it before. When you were newborn the immortal light shone thus in you. Recognize this. It is the evershining. Go gently into it and bathe in the energy that you once were. Do not be frightened or bewildered. Do not pull back in fear from the immensity of your true being. This is the time of your liberation.

My friend, maintain your open-heartedness, the spaciousness of your being that does not grasp. Let things be as they are without the least attempt to interfere. The angel *Michael* [Wonder] is on your right hand side, on your left is *Gavriel* [Strength], in front of you is *Uriel* [Light], and behind you is *Rafael* [Healing]. Above your head and surrounding you is *Shechinat-EI*, the Divine Presence.

The light that shines from the open heart of God shines for you with fullness now. The pure light of wisdom is finally available to you. The compassionate power of motherly understanding flows to you. My friend, do not cling to peaceful or painful states of mind. Allow yourself lovingly to let go of whatever resistance may have held you back.

Let the ground of your being flow smoothly from one world into the next. In each moment, within each object, within each image, the One exists. You are not isolated. On the contrary, your being is more in contact with us all. Remember to bless and help us, those you have loved. If you can weigh the scales on our behalf, do not hesitate. Let us know what your needs are, if we can somehow help you, and let us know if you are well. I open my dreams to you. Speak to me.

If feelings of anger or fear arise, recognize these obstructions to your essential freedom. Let go of frustration and fear. Let go of remorse and self-judgment. These are passing moods which float like clouds through the vast sky of your awareness. Do not be wearied as you travel through these shining realms. You are becoming like the essence of awareness itself.

My friend, you see now that even death does not exist. That who you are, awareness itself, does not depend upon a body for its existence. Float free in the vast spaciousness. Your devotion to the truth will carry you through. Move with open-heartedness toward the Light. Become the pure edgeless spaciousness within which the flow continues.

My friend, days will continue to pass after you have left your body. Know the truth as it is and move on, taking refuge in the vastness of your original nature. Know that you are well guided by your compassion and love. You are with the essence of all things. You are finally with the light. Amen.

Awake O north wind, come thou south, blow into your garden that your spices may flow out.

(Rabbi David Wolfe-Blank z"l)

Lentil

"For mourning is a sphere
Making a circuit in the world"—*
So do not be surprised when it appears
next door or even nearer.

And what shall we eat for mourning
but a lentil round as a mouth
that is closed—

What shall we say to them on the morning of a day
when no words are good, only
the touch of a hand, an embrace?

See them there: one silent, one shuddering
making one body of two, a perfect round.

(Rodger Kamenetz)

---

* Rashi on Bereshit 25:30: Jacob cooked lentils to provide the first meal to the mourner.
And why lentils? For they resemble a sphere, for mourning is a sphere making a circuit in the world.

Shiva

What is *Shiva?*

Shiva is a Hebrew word meaning "seven." The first seven days after a funeral are known as "*shiva*," and those who are mourning are said to be "sitting *shiva*." After a funeral, mourners stay at home — traditionally, for seven full days — and are fed, nurtured and cared-for by friends, neighbors and members of the community.

Shiva begins as the mourner departs from the cemetery, if there is a burial. It is customary to wash hands either upon exiting the cemetery or before arriving at the house of mourning, or both times. Friends or family often set out a pitcher of water and towels. After entering the home, the mourner may be encouraged to eat a meal of consolation. Perhaps food is not of interest to the bereaved. However, our tradition compels us to sustain life, returning to the world of living with breath, food and prayer. Long established custom across Jewish cultures and traditions is to eat foods that are round, recalling the roundness of the earth and the cycles of life. Some eat bagels, hard boiled eggs, chickpeas or lentils. Again, family or friends should prepare the table for the mourner and clean up as well so as to relieve the mourner of any burdens.

The custom of visiting mourners during *shiva* arose at a moment in time when it was presumed that everyone (or at least, all men) felt obligated in the *mitzvah* of daily communal prayer. To ensure that the mourners didn't need to leave their homes in order to find a *minyan* (a quorum of ten adult Jews) with which to pray, the community brings the *minyan* to them.

The first week of mourning gives the mourners time to come to grips with the reality of their loss, and time to grieve. It can be an emotionally and spiritually intense time. It is the job of the community to respond with love and compassion, to be helpful and generous. The most important thing anyone can do is to show up.

In many communities today, many people choose to observe formal *shiva* only for a few days, or for a single night. And for some of us who don't feel connected with a community, the first week after the funeral may be a time when that lack of connection is keenly felt precisely because the customs of *shiva* presume that community members will visit those who mourn.

The job of a mourner is to be present to their experience and their emotions. The job of those who come to *shiva* is to accompany the mourners, to bring them food, to listen when they need to talk, and to share memories of the person who has died. Those who do not have the comfort of community (or who do not find the presence of community to be a comfort) can still sit *shiva*.

The first week after a burial can be a time unlike any other in your life. Whatever emotions you feel, know that they are legitimate and they are real. May the customs of *shiva* be a comfort to you as you walk this road.

Customs of *Shiva*

There are many customs of *shiva*, and many different ways to experience the first week after burial. One of the most common customs is not to go to work — in fact, not even to leave the house — but instead to stay home and focus inward on the work of remembrance and mourning.

Some people follow the custom of covering their mirrors during this week. One explanation for this is to serve as a reminder not to focus on vanity, and instead to turn our focus inward to heart, soul, and memory. Others see it as remembrance of a folk custom that holds that the spirit of the deceased lingers among us; because spirits do not have a reflection in the mirror, we cover the mirror so that the soul of the deceased will not be "shamed" by its lack of body.

Another common custom of *shiva* is sitting on the ground, or on low stools or benches close to the ground: a reminder that we are embodied beings who can take comfort in the nearness of our mother, the Earth. Another is eschewing leather shoes or belts, or any garment that required the death of an animal in order to be fashioned. (Some observe this prohibition on Yom Kippur as well, which can be regarded as a day of rehearsal for our own deaths.) In another interpretation of this custom, we wear soft shoes during *shiva* as a reminder to maintain soft hearts, to be permeable and present to the range of emotions at this time.

May whatever customs of *shiva* you follow provide structure and comfort for you as you navigate these tender days.

Minchah / Afternoon Prayer

Lighting the *Shiva* Candle for the First Time

May the light of this candle gleam like the soul of _____.
May the light of this candle bring me comfort and keep me company.
And when this candle is gone, may the memory of _____
continue to illuminate my days.

יהוה אוֹרִי וְיִשְׁעִי, מִמִּי אִירָא? יהוה   ori v'yishi, mimi ira?
יהוה מָעוֹז חַיַּי, מִמִּי אֶפְחָד? יהוה   maoz-chayai, mimi efchad?

If יהוה is my light and my redemption, what shall I fear?
If יהוה is the strength of my life, what shall make me afraid?

(Psalm 27:1)

שְׁמַע יִשְׂרָאֵל, **Sh'ma, Yisra·el,**
יהוה אֱלֹהֵינוּ, יהוה אֶחָד. יהוה   Eloheinu, יהוה Echad.

Hear, O Israel, יהוה is our God, יהוה is One.

Ashrei
Short Chant

אַשְׁרֵי יוֹשְׁבֵי בֵיתֶךָ, עוֹד יְהַלְלוּךָ סֶּלָה׃

Ashrei yosh'vei veitecha, od y'hal'lucha selah.

Happy are they who dwell in Your house, they will praise You forever.

Full-Text Ashrei

אַשְׁרֵי יוֹשְׁבֵי בֵיתֶךָ,	Ashrei yosh'vei veitecha
עוֹד יְהַלְלוּךָ סֶּלָה׃	od y'hal'lucha selah.
אַשְׁרֵי הָעָם שֶׁכָּכָה לּוֹ,	Ashrei haam shekacha lo,
אַשְׁרֵי הָעָם שֶׁיהוה אֱלֹהָיו׃	Ashrei haam she-יהוה Elohav.
תְּהִלָּה לְדָוִד,	T'hilah l'David.
אֲרוֹמִמְךָ אֱלוֹהַי הַמֶּלֶךְ,	Aromimcha Elohai haMelech
וַאֲבָרְכָה שִׁמְךָ לְעוֹלָם וָעֶד׃	vaavarcha shimcha l'olam va·ed.
בְּכָל יוֹם אֲבָרְכֶךָּ,	B'chol yom avarcheka,
וַאֲהַלְלָה שִׁמְךָ לְעוֹלָם וָעֶד׃	vaahal'la shimcha l'olam va·ed.
גָּדוֹל יהוה וּמְהֻלָּל מְאֹד,	Gadol יהוה umhulal m'od,
וְלִגְדֻלָּתוֹ אֵין חֵקֶר׃	v'ligdulato ein cheiker.
דּוֹר לְדוֹר יְשַׁבַּח מַעֲשֶׂיךָ,	Dor l'dor y'shabach maasecha,
וּגְבוּרֹתֶיךָ יַגִּידוּ׃	ugvurotecha yagidu.
הֲדַר כְּבוֹד הוֹדֶךָ,	Hadar k'vod hodecha,
וְדִבְרֵי נִפְלְאֹתֶיךָ אָשִׂיחָה׃	v'divrei nifl'otecha asichah.
וֶעֱזוּז נוֹרְאוֹתֶיךָ יֹאמֵרוּ,	Ve·ezuz nor'otecha yomeiru,
וּגְדֻלָּתְךָ אֲסַפְּרֶנָּה׃	ugdulat'cha asaprenah.
זֵכֶר רַב טוּבְךָ יַבִּיעוּ,	Zeicher rav tuv'cha yabi·u,
וְצִדְקָתְךָ יְרַנֵּנוּ׃	v'tzidkat'cha y'raneinu.
חַנּוּן וְרַחוּם יהוה,	Chanun v'rachum יהוה,
אֶרֶךְ אַפַּיִם וּגְדָל חָסֶד׃	erech apayim ugdol chased.
טוֹב יהוה לַכֹּל,	Tov יהוה lakol,
וְרַחֲמָיו עַל כָּל מַעֲשָׂיו׃	v'rachamav al kol maasav.
יוֹדוּךָ יהוה כָּל מַעֲשֶׂיךָ,	Yoducha יהוה kol maasecha,
וַחֲסִידֶיךָ יְבָרְכוּכָה׃	vachasidecha y'varchucha.
כְּבוֹד מַלְכוּתְךָ יֹאמֵרוּ,	K'vod malchut'cha yomeiru,
וּגְבוּרָתְךָ יְדַבֵּרוּ׃	ugvurat'cha y'dabeiru.

לְהוֹדִיעַ לִבְנֵי הָאָדָם גְּבוּרֹתָיו, L'hodia livnei haadam g'vurotav,
וּכְבוֹד הֲדַר מַלְכוּתוֹ. uchvod hadar malchuto.

מַלְכוּתְךָ מַלְכוּת כָּל עוֹלָמִים, Malchut'cha malchut kol olamim,
וּמֶמְשַׁלְתְּךָ בְּכָל דֹּר וָדֹר. umemshalt'cha b'chol dor vador.

סוֹמֵךְ יהוה לְכָל הַנֹּפְלִים, Someich יהוה l'chol hanoflim,
וְזוֹקֵף לְכָל הַכְּפוּפִים. v'zokeif l'chol hak'fufim.

עֵינֵי כֹל אֵלֶיךָ יְשַׂבֵּרוּ, Einei chol eilecha y'sabeiru,
וְאַתָּה נוֹתֵן לָהֶם אֶת אָכְלָם בְּעִתּוֹ. v'atah notein lahem et ochlam b'ito.

פּוֹתֵחַ אֶת יָדֶךָ, Potei·ach et yadecha,
וּמַשְׂבִּיעַ לְכָל חַי רָצוֹן. umasbi·a l'chol chai ratzon.

צַדִּיק יהוה בְּכָל דְּרָכָיו, Tzadik יהוה b'chol drachav,
וְחָסִיד בְּכָל מַעֲשָׂיו. v'chasid b'chol maasav.

קָרוֹב יהוה לְכָל קֹרְאָיו, Karov יהוה l'chol kor'av,
לְכֹל אֲשֶׁר יִקְרָאֻהוּ בֶאֱמֶת. l'chol asher yikra·uhu ve·emet.

רְצוֹן יְרֵאָיו יַעֲשֶׂה, R'tzon y'rei·av ya·aseh,
וְאֶת שַׁוְעָתָם יִשְׁמַע וְיוֹשִׁיעֵם. v'et shavatam yishma v'yoshi·eim.

שׁוֹמֵר יהוה אֶת כָּל אֹהֲבָיו, Shomeir יהוה et kol ohavav,
וְאֵת כָּל הָרְשָׁעִים יַשְׁמִיד. v'eit kol har'sha·im yashmid.

תְּהִלַּת יהוה יְדַבֶּר פִּי, T'hilat יהוה y'daber pi,
וִיבָרֵךְ כָּל בָּשָׂר vivareich kol basar
שֵׁם קָדְשׁוֹ לְעוֹלָם וָעֶד. sheim kodsho l'olam va·ed.

וַאֲנַחְנוּ נְבָרֵךְ יָהּ, Vaanachnu n'vareich Yah
מֵעַתָּה וְעַד עוֹלָם, mei·atah v'ad olam,
הַלְלוּיָהּ. hal'lu-Yah!

Full-Text Ashrei

Happy are they who dwell in Your house;
may they continue to praise You!

Happy is the people for whom life is thus;
happy is the people with the Everlasting for its God!

A Psalm of David:

All exaltations I raise to You; I bless Your name forever.
Blessings do I offer You each day; I hail Your name, forever!
Great is the Eternal, to be praised; God's greatness is boundless.
Declaring praises for Your deeds, we describe Your mighty acts.
Heaven's splendor is my song; words of Your miracles I sing.
Wondrous are Your powers; we tell of Your magnificence.
Signs of Your abundant goodness we express; in Your justice we rejoice.
Gracious and merciful are You; slow to anger, great in love.
To all God's creatures, goodness flows; on all creation, love.
Your creatures all give thanks to You and bless You.
Calling out Your sovereign glory, we speak Your magnificence.
Letting all know Your mighty acts, Your glory and splendor.
May Your sovereignty last all eternities, Your dominion forever.
Strong support to all who fall, God raises up the humble and lame.
All gazes turn toward You for sustenance in its appointed time.
Providing with Your open hand, You satisfy desire in all life.
So just is God in every way, so loving amid all the divine deeds.
Close by is God to all who call, to all who call to God in truth.
Responding to yearning and awe, God hears their cry and rescues.
Showing care to all who love God, God destroys evildoing.
The praise of God my mouth declares; all flesh blesses the Holy Name forever.
And as for us, we bless the name of Yah, from now until the end of time.
Halleluyah!

Renewed Ashrei

This variation on the Ashrei uses quotations from His Holiness The Dalai Lama to articulate the themes of the Ashrei. Like the classical Ashrei, it is an alphabetical acrostic.

If you want others to be happy, practice compassion.
If you want to be happy, practice compassion.

Account for the fact that great love / and great achievements involve great risk.
But when you lose at something you attempted / don't lose the lesson.
Chart by the three R's: / Respect for self, Respect for others and Responsibility.
Don't forget that not getting what you want / is sometimes a stroke of luck.
Each time you realize you've made a mistake / take immediate steps to correct it.
Friendships include differences / don't let a dispute injure a relationship.
Genuine friends will stand by you / whether you are successful or unlucky.
Happiness is not something ready-made. / It comes from your own actions.
In disagreements deal only with the current situation. / Don't bring up the past.
Judge success by what you gave up / in order to get what you wanted.
Keep an open heart / everyone needs to be loved.
Love and compassion are necessities. / Without them, humanity cannot survive.
Maintain a sincere attitude / be concerned that outcomes are fair.
Nurture a loving atmosphere in your home / it is the foundation for your life.
Open your arms to change / but don't let go of your values.
Please be gentle with the earth / it's the only planet we have.
Quit complaining about others / and spend more time making yourself better.
Remember that silence ... / ... is sometimes the best answer.
Share your knowledge wisely. / It is a way to achieve immortality.
Twice or even once a year / go someplace you've never been before.
Understanding for others / brings the tranquility and happiness we seek.
Verify your understanding / but don't forget to believe and have faith.
We all need some time alone / make room for you each and every day.
X-ray vision doesn't exist / but seeking the truth is a good start.
You are not alone / God made all of us unique but not special.
Zero in on what matters / and start each day with loving yourself.

(Rabbi Evan Krame)

The Kaddish: A Door

In all of its forms, the Kaddish is a doorway
between one part of the service and the next.

As we move through this door, notice:
what is happening in your heart and mind?

Whatever is arising in you,
bring that into your prayer.

Chatzi Kaddish / Half Kaddish

יִתְגַּדַּל וְיִתְקַדַּשׁ שְׁמֵהּ רַבָּא. **Yitgadal v'yitkadash** sh'meih raba.
בְּעָלְמָא דִּי בְרָא כִרְעוּתֵהּ, B'al'ma di v'ra chiruteih.
וְיַמְלִיךְ מַלְכוּתֵהּ, v'yamlich malchuteih
בְּחַיֵּיכוֹן וּבְיוֹמֵיכוֹן, b'chayeichon uvyomeichon,
וּבְחַיֵּי דְכָל בֵּית יִשְׂרָאֵל, uvchayei d'chol beit Yisra·el
בַּעֲגָלָא וּבִזְמַן קָרִיב; ba·agala uvizman kariv;
וְאִמְרוּ אָמֵן : v'imru: **Amen.**

יְהֵא שְׁמֵהּ רַבָּא מְבָרַךְ **Y'hei sh'meih raba m'varach**
לְעָלַם וּלְעָלְמֵי עָלְמַיָּא. **l'alam ulal'mei almaya.**

יִתְבָּרַךְ וְיִשְׁתַּבַּח וְיִתְפָּאַר Yitbarach v'yishtabach v'yitpa·ar
וְיִתְרוֹמַם וְיִתְנַשֵּׂא וְיִתְהַדָּר v'yit·romam v'yitnasei v'yit·hadar
וְיִתְעַלֶּה וְיִתְהַלָּל שְׁמֵהּ דְּקֻדְשָׁא v'yitaleh v'yit·halal sh'meih d'kudsha
בְּרִיךְ הוּא, b'rich Hu,
לְעֵלָּא l'eila

During the Ten Days of Repentance:
וּלְעֵלָּא uleila

מִן כָּל בִּרְכָתָא וְשִׁירָתָא min kol birchata v'shirata,
תֻּשְׁבְּחָתָא וְנֶחֱמָתָא, tushb'chata v'nechemata,
דַּאֲמִירָן בְּעָלְמָא, da·amiran b'al'ma,
וְאִמְרוּ אָמֵן. v'imru: **Amen.**

Magnified and sanctified! Magnified and sanctified!
May God's Great Name fill the world God created.
May God's splendor be seen in the world in your life,
in your days, in the life of all Israel. Quickly and soon!
And let us say, **Amen.**'

Forever may the Great Name be blessed!

Blessed and praised! Splendid and supreme!
May the holy Name, **Bless God**, be praised,
far beyond all the blessings and songs, comforts and consolations,
that can be offered in this world.
And let us say: **Amen.**

(Translator: Rabbi Daniel Brenner)

Shiviti

A *shiviti* is an image of a divine Name, designed for meditative focus as a way of fulfilling the verse from Psalm 16, "I keep God before me always." This one was illustrated by an artist known as *Ba·al HaKochav.* Gaze at it, and let your mind and heart focus on God, whatever that word means for you.

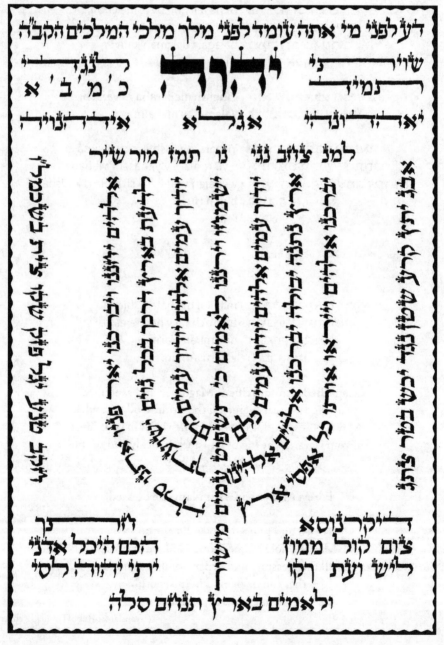

Weekday Amidah

There are two versions of the weekday Amidah, the standing prayer that is at the heart of every Jewish service. First there is a contemplative version, in which we offer a *kavanah* / meditative focus for each Amidah theme. Then there is the full-text version, which features the complete Hebrew text. Use whichever one best allows you to speak from your heart the words you most need to say to the One at this time.

The contemplative Amidah follows here. The full-text Amidah appears on p. 39.

Contemplative Amidah

These are the themes of the weekday Amidah. Meditate on each of them in your own time. If you wish to close each reflection with the closing words in Hebrew that "seal" each blessing, they are here for your use.

Avot V'imahot / Ancestors

I reflect on my ancestors. Who did I come from? How did they shape me?
Baruch atah, יהוה, magein Avraham v'ezrat Sarah.
בָּרוּךְ אַתָּה, יהוה, מָגֵן אַבְרָהָם וְעֶזְרַת שָׂרָה.

Gevurot / Power

What is the source of power in my life?
Where do I find strength? What enlivens me?
Baruch atah, יהוה, m'chayei hameitim.
בָּרוּךְ אַתָּה, יהוה, מְחַיֵּה הַמֵּתִים.

Kedushah / Holiness

I open myself to holiness. I seek to live wholly and in a way that is holy.
Baruch atah, יהוה, ha·el hakadosh.
בָּרוּךְ אַתָּה, יהוה, הָאֵל הַקָּדוֹשׁ.

Binah / Understanding

I seek wisdom and understanding in my life.
Baruch atah, יהוה, chonein hadaat.
בָּרוּךְ אַתָּה, יהוה, חוֹנֵן הַדָּעַת.

T'shuvah / Return

I want to orient myself in the right direction,
to re/turn to my deepest self and my highest aspirations.
Baruch atah, יהוה, harotzeh bit·shuvah.
בָּרוּךְ אַתָּה, יהוה, הָרוֹצֶה בִּתְשׁוּבָה.

S'licha / Forgiveness

I aspire to cultivate forgiveness, and I ask all those whom I have hurt to forgive me.

Baruch atah, יהוה, chanun hamarbeh lislo·ach.

בָּרוּךְ אַתָּה, יהוה, חַנּוּן הַמַּרְבֶּה לִסְלֹחַ.

Ge·ulah / Redemption

I ask the Source of transformation to lift me out of my narrow places.

Baruch atah, יהוה, go·eil Yisra·el.

בָּרוּךְ אַתָּה, יהוה, גּוֹאֵל יִשְׂרָאֵל.

Refuah / Healing

Heal my wounded places. Help me be a source of healing for others.

Baruch atah, יהוה, rofei cholei amo Yisra·el.

בָּרוּךְ אַתָּה, יהוה, רוֹפֵא חוֹלֵי עַמּוֹ יִשְׂרָאֵל.

Birkat Hashanim / Cycles

May abundant blessing pour into creation in this turning of the wheel
and in all of the cycles of our lives.

Baruch atah, יהוה, m'vareich hashanim.

בָּרוּךְ אַתָּה, יהוה, מְבָרֵךְ הַשָּׁנִים.

Kibutz Galuyot / Ingathering

May we be gathered in from our spiritual exile.
May this be true for us as individuals and for us as a people.

Baruch atah, יהוה, m'kabeitz nidchei amo Yisra·el.

בָּרוּךְ אַתָּה, יהוה, מְקַבֵּץ נִדְחֵי עַמּוֹ יִשְׂרָאֵל.

Din / Justice

May justice flow like waters
and righteousness like a mighty stream.
May we all be blessed with good judgment, discernment, and good boundaries.

Baruch atah, יהוה, Melech oheiv tz'dakah umishpat.

בָּרוּךְ אַתָּה, יהוה, מֶלֶךְ אוֹהֵב צְדָקָה וּמִשְׁפָּט.

Birkat Haminim / Divisions

May unhelpful divisions be bridged and healed.
May wickedness come to its end. May hope and righteousness reign.

Baruch atah, יהוה, shoveir oy'vim umachni·a zeidim.

בָּרוּךְ אַתָּה, יהוה, שֹׁבֵר אִיְבִים וּמַכְנִיעַ זֵדִים.

Tzadikim / Righteous Ones

May all of my righteous and holy teachers be blessed.
May I recognize that the whole world can be my teacher.
Baruch atah, יהוה, mishan umivtach latzadikim.

בָּרוּךְ אַתָּה, יהוה, מִשְׁעָן וּמִבְטָח לַצַּדִּיקִים.

Boneih Yerushalayim / Jerusalem

May Jerusalem, our holy city of old, be blessed with wholeness and peace.
May her inhabitants relate to one another with righteousness and love.
May all places where humanity dwells be blessed.
Baruch atah, יהוה, boneih Yerushalayim.

בָּרוּךְ אַתָּה, יהוה, בּוֹנֶה יְרוּשָׁלָיִם.

Y'shu·ah / A World Transformed

May redemption flower forth and transform our world
into a world where suffering, hatred, and loss are no more.
Baruch atah, יהוה, matzmi·ach keren y'shu·ah.

בָּרוּךְ אַתָּה, יהוה, מַצְמִיחַ קֶרֶן יְשׁוּעָה.

Sh'ma Koleinu / Hear Our Voices

May our prayers be heard on high and deep within.
May the deepest murmurings of our hearts be heard and honored.
Baruch atah, יהוה, shomei·a t'filah.

בָּרוּךְ אַתָּה, יהוה, שׁוֹמֵעַ תְּפִלָּה.

Avodah / Service

May my life be an expression of my desire to serve something greater than myself.
May my service help to uplift Shechinah, Divine presence, everywhere.
Baruch atah, יהוה, hamachazir shechinato l'tziyon.

בָּרוּךְ אַתָּה, יהוה, הַמַּחֲזִיר שְׁכִינָתוֹ לְצִיּוֹן.

Hoda·ah / Gratitude

Help me to cultivate gratitude for the blessings of every day.
Baruch atah, יהוה, hatov shimcha ulcha na·eh l'hodot.

בָּרוּךְ אַתָּה, יהוה, הַטּוֹב שִׁמְךָ וּלְךָ נָאֶה לְהוֹדוֹת.

Shalom / Peace

Help me to feel and to embody peace and wholeness.
Baruch atah, יהוה, hamvareich et amo Yisra·el bashalom.

בָּרוּךְ אַתָּה, יהוה, הַמְבָרֵךְ אֶת עַמּוֹ יִשְׂרָאֵל בַּשָּׁלוֹם.

עֹשֶׂה שָׁלוֹם בִּמְרוֹמָיו   Oseh shalom bimromav,
הוּא יַעֲשֶׂה שָׁלוֹם עָלֵינוּ   Hu ya·aseh shalom aleinu
וְעַל כָּל יִשְׂרָאֵל, וְעַל כָּל יוֹשְׁבֵי תֵבֵל,   v'al kol Yisra·el, v'al kol yosh'vei teiveil,
וְאִמְרוּ: אָמֵן.   v'imru: Amen.

May the One who makes peace in the heavens
make peace for us, for all Israel, and for all who dwell on earth.
And let us say: Amen.

Full-Text Amidah

אֲדֹנָי, שְׂפָתַי תִּפְתָּח, Adonai, s'fatai tiftach,
וּפִי יַגִּיד תְּהִלָּתֶךָ. ufi yagid t'hilatecha.

Eternal God, open my lips
that my mouth will declare Your praise.

Avot V'imahot / Ancestors

בָּרוּךְ אַתָּה, יהוה, אֱלֹהֵינוּ Baruch atah, יהוה, Eloheinu
וֵאלֹהֵי אֲבוֹתֵינוּ וְאִמּוֹתֵינוּ, veilohei avoteinu v'imoteinu,
אֱלֹהֵי אַבְרָהָם, אֱלֹהֵי יִצְחָק, Elohei Avraham, Elohei Yitzchak,
וֵאלֹהֵי יַעֲקֹב, Veilohei Ya·akov,

some omit

אלֹהֵי שָׂרָה, אלֹהֵי רִבְקָה, Elohei Sarah, Elohei Rivkah,
אלֹהֵי רָחֵל, וֵאלֹהֵי לֵאָה. Elohei Racheil, veilohei Lei·ah.

הָאֵל הַגָּדוֹל הַגִּבּוֹר וְהַנּוֹרָא, Ha·el hagadol hagibor v'hanora,
אֵל עֶלְיוֹן, El elyon,
גּוֹמֵל חֲסָדִים טוֹבִים, gomeil chasadim tovim
וְקֹנֵה הַכֹּל, v'koneih hakol
וְזוֹכֵר חַסְדֵי אָבוֹת וְאִמָּהוֹת, v'zocheir chasdei avot v'imahot,
וּמֵבִיא גוֹאֵל לִבְנֵי בְנֵיהֶם, umeivi go·eil livnei v'neihem,
לְמַעַן שְׁמוֹ בְּאַהֲבָה. l'ma·an sh'mo b'ahavah.

Blessed are You, יהוה, our God and God of our ancestors,
God of Abraham, God of Isaac, God of Jacob;
God of Sarah, God of Rebecca, God of Rachel and God of Leah;
the great, mighty, and awesome God,
God on high,
who does deeds of lovingkindness,
who is the Source of all,
and who remembers the steadfast love of our ancestors,
who lovingly brings redemption to their children's children
for Your name's sake.

During the Ten Days of Repentance (between Rosh Hashanah and Yom Kippur):

זָכְרֵנוּ לְחַיִּים,   Zochreinu l'chayim,

מֶלֶךְ חָפֵץ בַּחַיִּים,   melech chafeitz bachayim,

וְכָתְבֵנוּ בְּסֵפֶר הַחַיִּים,   v'chotveinu b'sefer hachayim,

לְמַעַנְךָ, אֱלֹהִים חַיִּים.   l'ma·ancha, Elohim chayim.

Remember us for life, Sovereign who chooses life, and inscribe us
in the book of life for Your sake, God of life.

מֶלֶךְ עוֹזֵר וּמוֹשִׁיעַ וּמָגֵן.   Melech ozeir umoshi·a umagein.

בָּרוּךְ אַתָּה, יהוה, מָגֵן אַבְרָהָם   Baruch atah, יהוה, magein Avraham

some omit

וְעֶזְרַת שָׂרָה.   v'ezrat Sarah.

Ruler, Helper, Redeemer, and Protector,
Blessed are You, Abraham's shield and Sarah's strength.

Gevurot / Strength

אַתָּה גִּבּוֹר לְעוֹלָם, יהוה,   Atah gibor l'olam, יהוה,

מְחַיֵּה מֵתִים אַתָּה, רַב לְהוֹשִׁיעַ.   m'chayei meitim atah, rav l'hoshi·a.

Summer:

מוֹרִיד הַטָּל.   Morid hatal.

Winter:

מַשִּׁיב הָרוּחַ וּמוֹרִיד הַגֶּשֶׁם.   Mashiv haru·ach umorid hageshem.

You are our eternal strength, יהוה.
Your saving power gives life that transcends death.

Summer: You bring the dew of the field.
Winter: You cause the winds to blow and the rains to fall.

מְכַלְכֵּל חַיִּים בְּחֶסֶד,   M'chalkeil chayim b'chesed,
מְחַיֵּה מֵתִים בְּרַחֲמִים רַבִּים,   m'chayeih meitim b'rachamim rabim,
סוֹמֵךְ נוֹפְלִים, וְרוֹפֵא חוֹלִים,   someich nof'lim, v'rofei cholim,
וּמַתִּיר אֲסוּרִים,   umatir asurim,
וּמְקַיֵּם אֱמוּנָתוֹ לִישֵׁנֵי עָפָר.   umkayeim emunato lisheinei afar.
מִי כָמוֹךָ בַּעַל גְּבוּרוֹת,   Mi chamocha, ba·al gevurot;
וּמִי דּוֹמֶה לָּךְ,   umi domeh lach,
מֶלֶךְ מֵמִית וּמְחַיֶּה   melech meimit umchayeh,
וּמַצְמִיחַ יְשׁוּעָה.   umatzmi·ach y'shu·ah.

You sustain the living with kindness,
in Your great mercy You bestow eternal life.
You support the fallen, heal the sick,
and free the captive.
You keep Your faith with us beyond life and death.
There is none like You, our Source of strength,
the ruler of life and death, the Source of our redemption.

During the Ten Days of Repentance (between Rosh Hashanah and Yom Kippur):

מִי כָמוֹךָ אַב הָרַחֲמִים,   Mi chamocha av harachamim,
זוֹכֵר יְצוּרָיו לְחַיִּים בְּרַחֲמִים.   zocheir y'tzurav l'chayim b'rachamim.

Who is like You, Merciful Parent? You remember us for life in compassion!

וְנֶאֱמָן אַתָּה לְהַחֲיוֹת מֵתִים.   V'ne·eman atah l'hachayot meitim.
בָּרוּךְ אַתָּה, יהוה, מְחַיֵּה הַמֵּתִים.   Baruch atah, יהוה, m'chayeih hameitim.

Our faith is with You, the God Who brings eternal life.
Blessed are You, יהוה, Who gives life that transcends death.

K'dushat HaShem / Sanctification of God's Name

(In the presence of a *minyan*, recite the following Kedushah:)

נְקַדֵּשׁ אֶת שִׁמְךָ בָּעוֹלָם,
N'kadeish et shimcha ba·olam;

כְּשֵׁם שֶׁמַּקְדִּישִׁים אוֹתוֹ
k'sheim shemakdishim oto

בִּשְׁמֵי מָרוֹם,
bishmei marom,

כַּכָּתוּב עַל יַד נְבִיאֶךָ:
kakatuv al yad n'vi·echa:

וְקָרָא זֶה אֶל זֶה וְאָמַר:
v'kara zeh el zeh v'amar:

קָדוֹשׁ, קָדוֹשׁ, קָדוֹשׁ,
Kadosh, kadosh, kadosh,

יהוה צְבָאוֹת,
יהוה tz'vaot,

מְלֹא כָל הָאָרֶץ כְּבוֹדוֹ.
m'lo chol haaretz k'vodo.

לְעֻמָּתָם בָּרוּךְ יֹאמֵרוּ:
L'umatam baruch yomeru:

בָּרוּךְ כְּבוֹד יהוה מִמְּקוֹמוֹ.
Baruch k'vod יהוה mim'komo.

וּבְדִבְרֵי קָדְשְׁךָ כָּתוּב לֵאמֹר:
Uvdivrei kodsh'kha katuv leimor:

יִמְלֹךְ יהוה לְעוֹלָם, אֱלֹהַיִךְ צִיּוֹן,
Yimloch יהוה l'olam, Elohayich Tziyon,

לְדֹר וָדֹר, הַלְלוּיָהּ.
ledor vador, hal'lu-Yah.

לְדוֹר וָדוֹר נַגִּיד גָּדְלֶךָ,
Ledor vador nagid godlecha,

וּלְנֵצַח נְצָחִים קְדֻשָּׁתְךָ נַקְדִּישׁ,
ulneitzach n'tzachim k'dushat'cha nakdish,

וְשִׁבְחֲךָ, אֱלֹהֵינוּ,
v'shivchacha, Eloheinu,

מִפִּינוּ לֹא יָמוּשׁ לְעוֹלָם וָעֶד,
mipinu lo yamush l'olam va·ed,

כִּי אֵל מֶלֶךְ גָּדוֹל וְקָדוֹשׁ אָתָּה.
ki El melech gadol v'kadosh atah.

*בָּרוּךְ אַתָּה, יהוה, הָאֵל הַקָּדוֹשׁ.
Baruch atah, יהוה, ha-El hakadosh.

---

*During the Ten Days of Repentance:

בָּרוּךְ אַתָּה, יהוה, הַמֶּלֶךְ הַקָּדוֹשׁ.   Baruch atah, יהוה, ha·Melech hakadosh.

(In the absence of a *minyan*, use this short kedushah instead:)

אַתָּה קָדוֹשׁ וְשִׁמְךָ קָדוֹשׁ,
Atah kadosh v'shimcha kadosh

וּקְדוֹשִׁים בְּכָל יוֹם יְהַלְלוּךָ סֶּלָה.
ukdoshim b'chol yom y'hal'lucha selah.

*בָּרוּךְ אַתָּה, יהוה, הָאֵל הַקָּדוֹשׁ.
Baruch atah, יהוה, ha-el hakadosh.

---

*During the Ten Days of Repentance:

בָּרוּךְ אַתָּה, יהוה, הַמֶּלֶךְ הַקָּדוֹשׁ.   Baruch atah, יהוה, ha·Melech hakadosh.

May Your name be sanctified in the world
as the angels sanctify
it in the heavens above.
As Your prophet wrote,
they cry out to one another:

Holy, holy, holy
is יהוה Tzevaot!
The whole earth is filled with Your glory!

And those who bless You say:
Blessed is the glory of יהוה from God's place.

And in Your holy words it is written:
May יהוה, your God, O Zion,
rule eternally from generation to generation. Hallelujah!

May each generation speak of Your greatness to the next.
For all eternity, may we sanctify Your holiness.
May Your praise, our God,
never depart from our lips,
for You are our great and holy God.
*Blessed are You, יהוה, the holy God.

*During the Ten Days of Repentance: Blessed are You, יהוה, the holy King.

(In the absence of a *minyan*, use this short kedushah instead:)

You are holy, and Your name is holy,
and holy ones praise You always.
*Blessed are You, יהוה, the holy God.

*During the Ten Days of Repentance: Blessed are You, יהוה, the holy King.

Bakashot / Weekday requests

אַתָּה חוֹנֵן לְאָדָם דַּעַת, Atah chonein l'adam da·at,
וּמְלַמֵּד לֶאֱנוֹשׁ בִּינָה. umlameid le·enosh binah.
חָנֵּנוּ מֵאִתְּךָ דֵעָה בִּינָה וְהַשְׂכֵּל. Choneinu mei·it'cha dei·ah binah v'haskeil.
בָּרוּךְ אַתָּה, יהוה, חוֹנֵן הַדָּעַת. Baruch atah, יהוה, chonein hadaat.

You give humanity wisdom and teach us understanding.
Grace us with knowledge, understanding, and discernment.
Blessed are You, יהוה, who graces us with wisdom.

הֲשִׁיבֵנוּ, אָבִינוּ, לְתוֹרָתֶךָ, Hashiveinu, avinu, l'toratecha,
וְקָרְבֵנוּ, מַלְכֵּנוּ, לַעֲבוֹדָתֶךָ, v'kar'veinu, malkeinu, la·avodatecha,
וְהַחֲזִירֵנוּ בִּתְשׁוּבָה שְׁלֵמָה לְפָנֶיךָ. v'hachazireinu bit·shuvah sh'leimah l'fanecha.
בָּרוּךְ אַתָּה, יהוה, הָרוֹצֶה בִּתְשׁוּבָה. Baruch atah, יהוה, harotzeh bit·shuvah,

Return us, our Parent, to Your Torah;
draw us near, our Sovereign, to Your service;
help us to return in complete t'shuvah before You.
Blessed are You, יהוה, who wishes for our t'shuvah.

סְלַח לָנוּ, אָבִינוּ, כִּי חָטָאנוּ; S'lach lanu, avinu, ki chatanu;
מְחַל לָנוּ, מַלְכֵּנוּ, כִּי פָשָׁעְנוּ, m'chal lanu, malkeinu, ki fashanu;
כִּי מוֹחֵל וְסוֹלֵחַ אָתָּה. ki mocheil v'solei·ach atah.
בָּרוּךְ אַתָּה, יהוה, Baruch atah, יהוה,
חַנּוּן הַמַּרְבֶּה לִסְלֹחַ. chanun hamarbeh lislo·ach.

Forgive us, our Parent, for we have sinned;
pardon us, our Sovereign, for we have erred;
for You are the one who forgives and pardons.
Blessed are You, יהוה, who graciously forgives.

רְאֵה נָא בְעָנְיֵנוּ, וְרִיבָה רִיבֵנוּ, R'eih na v'onyeinu, v'rivah riveinu,
וּגְאָלֵנוּ מְהֵרָה לְמַעַן שְׁמֶךָ, ugaleinu m'heira l'ma·an sh'mecha,
כִּי אֵל גּוֹאֵל חָזָק אָתָּה. ki El go·eil chazak atah.
בָּרוּךְ אַתָּה, יהוה, גּוֹאֵל יִשְׂרָאֵל. Baruch atah, יהוה, go·eil Yisra·el.

Take note of our affliction and our struggles.
Redeem us swiftly for Your name's sake.
Blessed are You, יהוה, Redeemer of Israel.

רְפָאֵנוּ, יהוה, וְנֵרָפֵא, הוֹשִׁיעֵנוּ   R'fa·einu, יהוה, v'neirafei, hoshi·einu
וְנִוָּשֵׁעָה, כִּי תְהִלָּתֵנוּ אָתָּה,   v'nivashei·ah, ki t'hilateinu atah,
וְהַעֲלֵה רְפוּאָה שְׁלֵמָה   v'ha·alei refu·ah sh'leimah
לְכָל מַכּוֹתֵינוּ. כִּי אֵל מֶלֶךְ רוֹפֵא   l'chol makoteinu. Ki El melech rofei
נֶאֱמָן וְרַחֲמָן אָתָּה. בָּרוּךְ אַתָּה יהוה,   ne·eman v'rachaman atah. Baruch atah, יהוה,
רוֹפֵא חוֹלֵי עַמּוֹ יִשְׂרָאֵל.   rofei cholei amo Yisra·el.

Heal us, יהוה, and we will be healed; save us, and we will be saved;
for You are the Healer, and, from You, complete healing rises for every wound.
Blessed are You, יהוה, Healer of the Sick among Your people.

בָּרֵךְ עָלֵינוּ, יהוה אֱלֹהֵינוּ,   Bareich aleinu, יהוה Eloheinu,
אֶת הַשָּׁנָה הַזֹּאת   et hashanah hazot
וְאֶת כָּל מִינֵי תְבוּאָתָהּ לְטוֹבָה,   v'et kol minei t'vu·atah l'tovah,

summer: וְתֵן בְּרָכָה   summer: v'tein b'rachah
winter: וְתֵן טַל וּמָטָר לִבְרָכָה   winter: v'tein tal umatar livrachah

עַל פְּנֵי הָאֲדָמָה, וְשַׂבְּעֵנוּ מִטּוּבָהּ,   al p'nei ha·adamah, v'sab'einu mituvah,
וּבָרֵךְ שְׁנָתֵנוּ כַּשָּׁנִים הַטּוֹבוֹת.   uvareich sh'nateinu kashanim hatovot.
בָּרוּךְ אַתָּה, יהוה, מְבָרֵךְ הַשָּׁנִים.   Baruch atah, יהוה, m'vareich hashanim.

Bless, יהוה our God, the cycle of this year
and all the various good things which grow.
in winter: Grant blessing
in summer: Grant the blessing of the dew
on the face of the earth.
Satisfy us with Your goodness, and bless this year as all good years.
Blessed are You, יהוה, who blesses the cycle of the years.

תְּקַע בְּשׁוֹפָר גָּדוֹל לְחֵרוּתֵנוּ,   T'ka b'shofar gadol l'cheiruteinu,
וְשָׂא נֵס לְקַבֵּץ גָּלֻיּוֹתֵינוּ,   v'sa neis l'kabeitz galuyoteinu,
וְקַבְּצֵנוּ יַחַד   v'kab'tzeinu yachad
מֵאַרְבַּע כַּנְפוֹת הָאָרֶץ.   mei·arba kanfot ha·aretz.
בָּרוּךְ אַתָּה, יהוה,   Baruch atah, יהוה,
מְקַבֵּץ נִדְחֵי עַמּוֹ יִשְׂרָאֵל.   m'kabeitz nidchei amo Yisra·el.

Sound the great shofar for our freedom; raise a banner for the oppressed;
gather us in from the four corners of the earth.
Blessed are You, יהוה, who ingathers the exiles of Your people.

הָשִׁיבָה שׁוֹפְטֵינוּ כְּבָרִאשׁוֹנָה   Hashivah shofteinu k'varishonah
וְיוֹעֲצֵינוּ כְּבַתְּחִלָּה,   v'yo·atzeinu k'vat'chilah,
וְהָסֵר מִמֶּנּוּ יָגוֹן וַאֲנָחָה,   v'haseir mimenu yagon va·anachah,
וּמְלוֹךְ עָלֵינוּ אַתָּה, יהוה,   umloch aleinu atah, יהוה,
לְבַדְּךָ בְּחֶסֶד וּבְרַחֲמִים,   levad·cha b'chesed uvrachamim,
וְצַדְּקֵנוּ בַּמִּשְׁפָּט.   v'tzad'keinu bamishpat.
בָּרוּךְ אַתָּה, יהוה,   Baruch atah, יהוה,
מֶלֶךְ אוֹהֵב צְדָקָה וּמִשְׁפָּט.   melech oheiv tz'dakah umishpat.

Let our judges be righteous, as they were of old;
bring mercy and lovingkindness through them;
for You are our ultimate Ruler, You alone in Your mercy and compassion,
Your justice and Your statutes.
Blessed are You, יהוה, Ruler who loves justice.

וְלַמַּלְשִׁינוּת אַל תְּהִי תִקְוָה,   V'lamalshinut al t'hi tikvah,
וְכָל הָרִשְׁעָה כְּרֶגַע תֹּאבֵד,   v'chol harishah k'rega toveid,
וְכָל אוֹיְבֶיךָ מְהֵרָה יִכָּרֵתוּ,   v'chol oy'vecha m'heira yikareitu,
וְהַזֵּדִים מְהֵרָה תְעַקֵּר וּתְשַׁבֵּר   v'hazeidim m'heira t'akeir ut·shabeir
וּתְמַגֵּר וְתַכְנִיעַ בִּמְהֵרָה בְיָמֵינוּ.   utmageir v'tachni·ah bimheira v'yameinu.
בָּרוּךְ אַתָּה, יהוה,   Baruch atah, יהוה,
שׁוֹבֵר אֹיְבִים וּמַכְנִיעַ זֵדִים.   shoveir oy'vim umachni·a zeidim.

And may wickedness not be given hope,
and may the errant return to You, speedily and in our days.
Blessed are You, יהוה, who shatters wickedness.

עַל הַצַּדִּיקִים וְעַל הַחֲסִידִים   Al hatzadikim v'al hachasidim
וְעַל זִקְנֵי עַמְּךָ בֵּית יִשְׂרָאֵל,   v'al ziknei am'cha beit Yisra·el,
וְעַל פְּלֵיטַת סוֹפְרֵיהֶם,   v'al p'leitat sof'reihem,
וְעַל גֵּרֵי הַצֶּדֶק וְעָלֵינוּ,   v'al geirei hatzedek v'aleinu,
יֶהֱמוּ נָא רַחֲמֶיךָ, יהוה אֱלֹהֵינוּ,   yehemu na rachamecha, יהוה Eloheinu,
וְתֵן שָׂכָר טוֹב לְכָל הַבּוֹטְחִים בְּשִׁמְךָ   v'tein sachar tov l'chol habot'chim b'shimcha
בֶּאֱמֶת, וְשִׂים חֶלְקֵנוּ עִמָּהֶם,   be·emet, v'sim chelkeinu imahem,
וּלְעוֹלָם לֹא נֵבוֹשׁ כִּי בְךָ בָּטָחְנוּ.   ulolam lo neivosh ki v'cha batachnu.
בָּרוּךְ אַתָּה, יהוה,   Baruch atah, יהוה,
מִשְׁעָן וּמִבְטָח לַצַּדִּיקִים.   mishan umivtach latzadikim.

And on the righteous ones and the pious ones and our elders,
and on our leaders, and on the strangers who dwell among us, and on us,
may You grant compassion, יהוה, our God, and give blessing and good reward to all
who trust in Your name, and number us among them forever,
and let us never waver from our faith in You.
Blessed are You, יהוה, the staff and stay of the righteous.

וְלִירוּשָׁלַיִם עִירְךָ בְּרַחֲמִים תָּשׁוּב, V'lirushalayim ir'cha b'rachamim tashuv,
וְתִשְׁכּוֹן בְּתוֹכָהּ כַּאֲשֶׁר דִּבַּרְתָּ, v'tishkon b'tochah ka·asher dibarta,
וּבְנֵה אוֹתָהּ בְּקָרוֹב בְּיָמֵינוּ uvneih otah b'karov b'yameinu
בִּנְיַן עוֹלָם, וְכִסֵּא דָוִד binyan olam, v'chisei David
מְהֵרָה לְתוֹכָהּ תָּכִין. m'heirah l'tochah tachin.
בָּרוּךְ אַתָּה, יהוה, בּוֹנֵה יְרוּשָׁלָיִם. Baruch atah, יהוה, boneih Yerushalayim.

And to Jerusalem, Your city, speedily return in compassion.
Help us to rebuild her speedily and in our days,
in a manner befitting the throne of David.
Give rest to Zion and help us to rebuild Jerusalem.
Blessed are You, יהוה, builder of Jerusalem.

אֶת צֶמַח דָּוִד עַבְדְּךָ מְהֵרָה Et tzemach David avd'cha m'heirah
תַצְמִיחַ, וְקַרְנוֹ תָּרוּם בִּישׁוּעָתֶךָ, tatzmi·ach, v'karno tarum bishu·atecha,
כִּי לִישׁוּעָתְךָ קִוִּינוּ כָּל הַיּוֹם. ki lishu·at'cha kivinu kol hayom.
בָּרוּךְ אַתָּה, יהוה, Baruch atah, יהוה,
מַצְמִיחַ קֶרֶן יְשׁוּעָה. matzmi·ach keren y'shu·ah.

May the sprout of David flower forth,
bringing with it Your redemption,
for we hope for Your redemption every day.
Blessed are You, יהוה, who brings forth redemption.

שְׁמַע קוֹלֵנוּ, יהוה אֱלֹהֵינוּ, Sh'ma koleinu, יהוה Eloheinu,
חוּס וְרַחֵם עָלֵינוּ, chus v'racheim aleinu,
וְקַבֵּל בְּרַחֲמִים וּבְרָצוֹן v'kabeil b'rachamim uvratzon
אֶת תְּפִלָּתֵנוּ, כִּי אֵל שׁוֹמֵעַ et t'filateinu, ki El shomei·a
תְּפִלּוֹת וְתַחֲנוּנִים אָתָּה, t'filot v'tachanunim atah,
וּמִלְּפָנֶיךָ, מַלְכֵּנוּ, umil'fanecha, Malkeinu,
רֵיקָם אַל תְּשִׁיבֵנוּ. כִּי אַתָּה שׁוֹמֵעַ reikam al t'shiveinu. Ki atah shomei·a
תְּפִלַּת עַמְּךָ יִשְׂרָאֵל בְּרַחֲמִים. t'filat am'cha Yisra·el b'rachamim.
בָּרוּךְ אַתָּה, יהוה, שׁוֹמֵעַ תְּפִלָּה. Baruch atah, יהוה, shomei·a t'filah.

Hear our words, יהוה our God, be compassionate and merciful upon us, and let our prayers be received with mercy according to Your will, for You are the one who hears our prayers and supplications which arise before You. You are the one who hears the prayers of Your people Israel with compassion. Blessed are You, יהוה, hearer of prayer.

רְצֵה, יהוה, אֱלֹהֵינוּ,	R'tzeih, יהוה, Eloheinu,
בְּעַמְּךָ יִשְׂרָאֵל, וְלִתְפִלָּתָם שְׁעֵה,	b'am'cha Yisra·el, v'litfilatam sh'ei,
וְהָשֵׁב אֶת הָעֲבוֹדָה לִדְבִיר בֵּיתֶךָ,	v'hasheiv et haavodah lidvir beitecha,
וְאִשֵּׁי יִשְׂרָאֵל, וּתְפִלָּתָם	v'ishei Yisra·el, utfilatam
מְהֵרָה בְּאַהֲבָה תְקַבֵּל בְּרָצוֹן,	m'heirah b'ahavah t'kabeil b'ratzon,
וּתְהִי לְרָצוֹן תָּמִיד	ut·hi l'ratzon tamid
עֲבוֹדַת יִשְׂרָאֵל עַמֶּךָ.	avodat Yisra·el amecha.
וְתֶחֱזֶינָה עֵינֵינוּ בְּשׁוּבְךָ לְצִיּוֹן	V'techezenah eineinu b'shuv'cha l'Tziyon
בְּרַחֲמִים. בָּרוּךְ אַתָּה, יהוה,	b'rachamim. Baruch atah, יהוה,
הַמַּחֲזִיר שְׁכִינָתוֹ לְצִיּוֹן.	hamachazir Shechinato letziyon.

Accept, יהוה, our God, the prayers of Your people Israel;
find favor in us and accept our prayers in love.
May our prayers always ascend to You in love.
And help our eyes and hearts to behold Your return to Zion with compassion.
Blessed are You, יהוה, whose presence returns always to Zion.

On Rosh Chodesh, and on the intermediate days of festivals:

אֱלֹהֵינוּ וֵאלֹהֵי אֲבוֹתֵינוּ וְאִמּוֹתֵינוּ
Eloheinu veilohei avoteinu v'imoteinu,

יַעֲלֶה וְיָבֹא, וְיַגִּיעַ, וְיֵרָאֶה,
ya·aleh v'yavo, v'yagi·a, v'yeira·eh,

וְיֵרָצֶה, וְיִשָּׁמַע, וְיִפָּקֵד,
v'yeiratzeh, v'yishama, v'yipakeid,

וְיִזָּכֵר זִכְרוֹנֵנוּ וּפִקְדוֹנֵנוּ,
v'yizacheir zichroneinu ufikdoneinu,

וְזִכְרוֹן אֲבוֹתֵינוּ וְאִמּוֹתֵינוּ,
v'zichron avoteinu v'imoteinu,

וְזִכְרוֹן מָשִׁיחַ בֶּן דָּוִד עַבְדֶּךָ,
v'zichron mashi·ach ben David avdecha,

וְזִכְרוֹן יְרוּשָׁלַיִם עִיר קָדְשֶׁךָ,
vzichron Yerushalayim ir kodshecha,

וְזִכְרוֹן כָּל עַמְּךָ בֵּית יִשְׂרָאֵל לְפָנֶיךָ,
v'zichron kol am'cha beit Yisra·el l'fanecha,

לִפְלֵיטָה, לְטוֹבָה,
lifleitah, l'tovah,

לְחֵן וּלְחֶסֶד וּלְרַחֲמִים,
l'chein ulchesed ulrachamim,

לְחַיִּים וּלְשָׁלוֹם,
l'chayim ulshalom,

בְּיוֹם
b'yom

לראש חדש: רֹאשׁ הַחֹדֶשׁ הַזֶּה.
Rosh Chodesh: Rosh haChodesh hazeh.

לפסח: חַג הַמַּצּוֹת הַזֶּה.
Pesach: Chag haMatzot hazeh.

לסכות: חַג הַסֻּכּוֹת הַזֶּה.
Sukkot: Chag haSukkot hazeh.

זָכְרֵנוּ, יהוה, אֱלֹהֵינוּ,
Zochreinu, יהוה, Eloheinu,

בּוֹ לְטוֹבָה,
bo l'tovah,

וּפָקְדֵנוּ בוֹ לִבְרָכָה,
ufokdeinu vo livrachah,

וְהוֹשִׁיעֵנוּ בוֹ לְחַיִּים,
v'hoshi·einu vo l'chayim,

וּבִדְבַר יְשׁוּעָה וְרַחֲמִים,
uvidvar y'shu·ah v'rachamim,

חוּס וְחָנֵּנוּ,
chus v'choneinu,

וְרַחֵם עָלֵינוּ
v'racheim aleinu

וְהוֹשִׁיעֵנוּ,
v'hoshi·einu,

כִּי אֵלֶיךָ עֵינֵינוּ,
ki eilecha eineinu,

כִּי אֵל מֶלֶךְ חַנּוּן וְרַחוּם אָתָּה.
ki El melech chanun v'rachum atah.

On Rosh Chodesh, and on the intermediate days of festivals:

Our God and God of our ancestors:
allow memory to ascend,
to come, to reach us.
May our memory
and our ancestors' memory
and the memory of the dream
of a messianic time,
and the memory of the vision
of Jerusalem as a city of peace,
and the memories of all of Your people
of the House of Israel,
be before You

on this day of (Rosh Chodesh) (Pesach) (Sukkot).

On this day,
may these memories,
these dreams of redemption,
inspire graciousness, lovingkindness,
and compassion in us,
for life and for peace.
Remember us, יהוה, our God, for goodness.
Count us in for blessing.
Save us with life.
Shower us with salvation
and with compassion;
be merciful to us; enfold us
in the compassion we knew
before we were born.
For You are our merciful Parent and Sovereign.

מוֹדִים אֲנַחְנוּ לָךְ, שָׁאַתָּה הוּא,   Modim anachnu lach, sha·atah hu,
יהוה אֱלֹהֵינוּ וֵאלֹהֵי אֲבוֹתֵינוּ   יהוה Eloheinu veilohei avoteinu
וְאִמּוֹתֵינוּ,   v'imoteinu,
לְעוֹלָם וָעֶד, צוּרֵנוּ צוּר חַיֵּינוּ,   l'olam va·ed, tzureinu tzur chayeinu,
מָגֵן יִשְׁעֵנוּ,   magein yisheinu,
אַתָּה הוּא לְדוֹר וָדוֹר,   atah hu l'dor vador,
נוֹדֶה לְּךָ וּנְסַפֵּר תְּהִלָּתֶךָ,   nodeh l'cha unsaper t'hilatecha,
עַל חַיֵּינוּ הַמְּסוּרִים בְּיָדֶךָ,   al chayeinu ham'surim b'yadecha,
וְעַל נִשְׁמוֹתֵינוּ הַפְּקוּדוֹת לָךְ,   v'al nishmoteinu hap'kudot lach,
וְעַל נִסֶּיךָ שֶׁבְּכָל יוֹם עִמָּנוּ,   v'al nisecha sheb'chol yom imanu,
וְעַל נִפְלְאוֹתֶיךָ וְטוֹבוֹתֶיךָ   v'al nifl'otecha v'tovotecha
שֶׁבְּכָל עֵת, עֶרֶב וָבֹקֶר וְצָהֳרָיִם: sheb'chol eit, erev vavoker v'tzohorayim:
הַטּוֹב, כִּי לֹא כָלוּ רַחֲמֶיךָ,   hatov, ki lo chalu rachamecha,
וְהַמְרַחֵם, כִּי לֹא תַמּוּ חֲסָדֶיךָ,   v'hamracheim, ki lo tamu chasadecha,
כִּי מֵעוֹלָם קִוִּינוּ לָךְ.   ki mei·olam kivinu lach.

We are grateful before You,
for You, יהוה our God and God of our ancestors, are forever
the Rock of our lives, the shield of our salvation.
You are this for us in every generation.
For our lives which are in Your hands,
and our souls which are in Your keeping,
and for the wonders You do for us each day
and the miracles You perform for us at every moment,
evening and morning and afternoon:
Your mercies never end;
Your compassion never fails;
we put our hope in You.

On Chanukah and Purim:

עַל הַנִּסִּים, וְעַל הַפֻּרְקָן,
וְעַל הַגְּבוּרוֹת, וְעַל הַתְּשׁוּעוֹת,
וְעַל הַנִּפְלָאוֹת,
שֶׁעָשִׂיתָ לַאֲבוֹתֵינוּ וּלְאִמּוֹתֵינוּ
בַּיָּמִים הָהֵם בַּזְּמַן הַזֶּה.

Al hanisim, v'al hapurkan,
v'al hag'vurot, v'al hat'shu·ot,
v'al hanifla·ot,
she·asita la·avoteinu ulimoteinu
bayamim haheim baz'man hazeh.

For the miracles, for the redemption,
for the mighty deeds, for the saving acts,
and for the wonders, which You wrought for our ancestors
in those days, at this time.

On Chanukah:

בִּימֵי מַתִּתְיָהוּ כֹּהֵן גָּדוֹל
חַשְׁמוֹנַאי וּבָנָיו כְּשֶׁעָמְדָה עֲלֵיהֶם
מַלְכוּת אַנְטִיּוֹכוֹס הָרָשָׁע
וּבִקֵּשׁ לַעֲקוֹר אֶת אֱמוּנָתֵינוּ
וְדָתֵנוּ וְהֵצֵרוּ לָנוּ וְכָבְשׁוּ אֶת
הֵיכָלֵינוּ טִמְּאוּ אֶת מִקְדָּשֵׁנוּ.
אָז קָמוּ נֶגְדָּם חֲסִידֶיךָ
וְכֹהֲנֶיךָ, וְאַתָּה, בְּרַחֲמֶיךָ
הָרַבִּים, עָמַדְתָּ לָהֶם בְּעֵת צָרָתָם,
רַבְתָּ אֶת רִיבָם, נָקַמְתָּ אֶת
נִקְמָתָם, וְהָיִיתָ בְּעֶזְרָתָם לְהִתְגַּבֵּר
עֲלֵיהֶם וּלְטַהֵר אֶת הַמִּקְדָּשׁ.
מִתּוֹךְ גַּעֲגוּעִים לְהַשְׁרָאָתְךָ
רָצוּ לְהַדְלִיק אֶת הַמְּנוֹרָה
הַטְּהוֹרָה וְלֹא מָצְאוּ שֶׁמֶן
עַד שֶׁהֶרְאֵיתָ לָהֶם שֶׁמֶן טָהוֹר
לְיוֹם אֶחָד. בְּבִטָּחוֹן הִדְלִיקוּ
אֶת הַמְּנוֹרָה וְאַתָּה עָשִׂיתָ לָהֶם
נֵס וָפֶלֶא, וְהַשֶּׁמֶן לֹא הִפְסִיק
עַד שֶׁעָשׂוּ מֵחָדָשׁ.
וְקָבְעוּ שְׁמוֹנַת יְמֵי חֲנֻכָּה
אֵלּוּ לְהַדְלִיק נֵרוֹת לְפִרְסוּם הַנֵּס
לְהוֹדוֹת בְּהַלֵּל לְשִׁמְךָ הַגָּדוֹל
וְהַקָּדוֹשׁ עַל נִסֶּיךָ
וְעַל נִפְלְאוֹתֶךָ וְעַל יְשׁוּעָתֶךָ.

Bimei Mattityahu kohein gadol
chashmonai uvanav k'she·amd'ah aleihem
malchut Antiyochos harasha
uvikeish la·akor et emunateinu
v'dateinu v'heitzeiru lanu v'chav'shu et
heichaleinu tim'u et mikdasheinu.
Az kamu negdam chasidecha
v'chohanecha, v'atah, b'rachamecha
harabim, amadta lahem b'eit tzaratam,
ravta et rivam, nakamta et
nikmatam, v'hayita b'ezratam l'hitgabeir
aleihem ultaheir et hamikdash.
Mitoch ga·agu·im l'hashra·at'cha
ratzu l'hadlik et hamenorah
hat'horah v'lo matz'u shemen
ad shehereita lahem shemen tahor
l'yom echad. B'vitachon hidliku
et hamenorah v'atah asita lahem
neis vafeleh v'hashemen lo hifsik
ad she·asu meichadash.
V'kav'u sh'monat y'mei chanukah
eilu l'hadlik neirot l'firsum haneis
l'hodot b'hallel l'shimcha hagadol
v'hakadosh al nisecha
v'al nifl'otecha v'al y'shu·atecha.

On Chanukah:

In the days of Mattityahu, High priest, and his sons, when there arose against them the reign of wicked Antiochus, who sought to uproot our faith and law, oppressing us, they conquered our Temple and desecrated our sanctuary. Then there arose, against them, Your devout priests, and You, in Your great compassion, stood by them, in their troubles, waging their wars, avenging their pain, helping them to overcome Antiochus' forces and to purify the sanctuary. Amidst their longing for Your Presence among them, they sought to kindle the pure lamp and, not finding enough pure oil, You led them to find some, just enough for one day. In trust, they kindled the lamp, and You miraculously made the oil last until they could make some afresh. Then did they set these days of Chanukah to lighting candles, to chanting the Hallel, in gratitude to Your great reputation for Your miracles, Your wonders, and Your salvation.

(Adaptation and translation by Rabbi Zalman Schachter-Shalomi z"l)

On Purim:

בִּימֵי מָרְדְּכַי וְאֶסְתֵּר בְּשׁוּשַׁן
הַבִּירָה, כְּשֶׁעָמַד עֲלֵיהֶם הָמָן
הָרָשָׁע, בִּקֵּשׁ לְהַשְׁמִיד,
לַהֲרֹג וּלְאַבֵּד אֶת כָּל הַיְּהוּדִים,
מִנַּעַר וְעַד זָקֵן, טַף וְנָשִׁים,
בְּיוֹם אֶחָד בִּשְׁלֹשָׁה עָשָׂר לְחֹדֶשׁ
שְׁנֵים עָשָׂר,
הוּא חֹדֶשׁ אֲדָר, וּשְׁלָלָם לָבוֹז.
וְאַתָּה בְּרַחֲמֶיךָ הָרַבִּים
הֵפַרְתָּ אֶת עֲצָתוֹ,
וְקִלְקַלְתָּ אֶת מַחֲשַׁבְתּוֹ,
וַהֲשֵׁבוֹתָ לוֹ גְּמוּלוֹ בְּרֹאשׁוֹ.

Bimei Mordechai v'Ester b'Shushan
habirah, k'she·amad aleihem Haman
harasha, bikeish l'hashmid,
laharog ulabeid et kol haihudim,
mina·ar v'ad zakein, taf v'nashim,
b'yom echad bishlosha asar l'chodesh
sh'neim asar,
hu chodesh Adar, ushlalam lavoz.
V'atah b'rachamecha harabim
heifarta et atzato,
v'kilkalta et mach·shavto,
vahasheivota lo g'mulo b'rosho.

In the days of Mordechai and Esther in Shushan, the capital,
when the wicked Haman arose before them and sought to destroy,
to slay, and to exterminate all the Jews —
young and old, infants and women
— on the same day, the thirteenth of the twelfth month,
which is the month of Adar, and to plunder their possessions:
You, in Your abundant mercy, nullified his counsel and frustrated his intention
and caused his design to return upon his own head.

וְעַל כֻּלָּם יִתְבָּרַךְ וְיִתְרוֹמַם   V'al kulam yitbarach v'yit·romam
שִׁמְךָ מַלְכֵּנוּ   shimcha Malkeinu
תָּמִיד לְעוֹלָם וָעֶד,   tamid l'olam va·ed,

For all these things, O God, let Your name forever be praised.

During the Ten Days of Repentance:

וּכְתֹב לְחַיִּים טוֹבִים כָּל בְּנֵי בְרִיתֶךָ,   uchtov l'chayim tovim kol b'nei v'ritecha,

May all the children of Your covenant be inscribed for a life of goodness,

וְכֹל הַחַיִּים יוֹדוּךָ סֶּלָה,   v'chol hachayim yoducha selah,
וִיהַלְלוּ אֶת שִׁמְךָ   vihal'lu et shimcha
בֶּאֱמֶת,   be·emet,
הָאֵל יְשׁוּעָתֵנוּ וְעֶזְרָתֵנוּ סֶּלָה.   ha·El y'shu·ateinu v'ezrateinu selah.
בָּרוּךְ אַתָּה, יהוה,   Baruch atah, יהוה,
הַטּוֹב שִׁמְךָ וּלְךָ נָאֶה לְהוֹדוֹת.   hatov shimcha ulcha na·eh l'hodot.

for You are the God of our redemption and our hope.
Blessed are You, יהוה, whose Name is good
and who does great things worthy of our thanksgiving.

שָׁלוֹם רָב עַל יִשְׂרָאֵל עַמְּךָ   Shalom rav al Yisra·el am'cha
תָּשִׂים לְעוֹלָם,   tasim l'olam,
כִּי אַתָּה הוּא   ki atah hu
מֶלֶךְ אָדוֹן לְכָל הַשָּׁלוֹם.   melech adon l'chol hashalom.
וְטוֹב בְּעֵינֶיךָ לְבָרֵךְ   V'tov b'einecha l'vareich
אֶת עַמְּךָ יִשְׂרָאֵל   et am'cha Yisra·el
בְּכָל עֵת וּבְכָל שָׁעָה בִּשְׁלוֹמֶךָ.   b'chol eit uv'chol sha·ah bishlomecha.

Grant abundant peace to Your people Israel always,
for You are the Sovereign of all peace.
May it be pleasing in Your eyes
to bless Your people Israel
in every season and moment with Your peace.

During the Ten Days of Repentance

בְּסֵפֶר חַיִּים, בְּרָכָה וְשָׁלוֹם,   B'sefer chayim, b'rachah, v'shalom,

וּפַרְנָסָה טוֹבָה, נִזָּכֵר וְנִכָּתֵב לְפָנֶיךָ,   ufarnasah tova, nizacheir v'nikateiv l'fanecha,

אֲנַחְנוּ וְכָל עַמְּךָ בֵּית יִשְׂרָאֵל,   anachnu v'chol am'cha beit Yisra·el,

לְחַיִּים טוֹבִים וּלְשָׁלוֹם.   l'chayim tovim ulshalom.

In the book of life, blessing, peace, and prosperity,
may we be remembered and inscribed by You,
— we and all Your people Israel —
for a good life and for peace.

בָּרוּךְ אַתָּה, יהוה, הַמְבָרֵךְ   Baruch atah, יהוה, hamvareich

אֶת עַמּוֹ יִשְׂרָאֵל בַּשָּׁלוֹם.   et amo Yisra·el bashalom.

Blessed are You, יהוה, who blesses Your people Israel with peace.

עֹשֶׂה שָׁלוֹם בִּמְרוֹמָיו,   Oseh shalom bimromav,

הוּא יַעֲשֶׂה שָׁלוֹם עָלֵינוּ   Hu ya·aseh shalom aleinu

וְעַל כָּל יִשְׂרָאֵל,   v'al kol Yisra·el,

וְעַל כָּל יוֹשְׁבֵי תֵבֵל,   v'al kol yosh'vei teiveil,

וְאִמְרוּ: אָמֵן.   v'imru: Amen.

May the One who makes peace in the heavens
make peace for us,
for all Israel,
and for all who dwell on earth.
And let us say: Amen.

Accept Our Offerings

We come together
    sometimes in gladness
        and sometimes in grief.

Sometimes with guilt,
    sometimes ambivalence.
        We come together

with hearts that may be
    broken, or embittered,
        or uncertain how to feel.

We come together
    though we may not know
        what to say, or how to say it.

Accept our offerings
    whatever they are.
        Help us to know

You don't ask pretense.
    You welcome every heart.
        Receive us, all our parts.

(Rabbi Rachel Barenblat)

The Kaddish: A Door

In all of its forms, the Kaddish is a doorway
between one part of the service and the next.

As we move through this door, notice:
what is happening in your heart and mind?

Whatever is arising in you,
bring that into your prayer.

Chatzi Kaddish / Half Kaddish

יִתְגַּדַּל וְיִתְקַדַּשׁ שְׁמֵהּ רַבָּא,
Yitgadal v'yitkadash sh'meih raba,

בְּעָלְמָא דִּי בְרָא כִרְעוּתֵהּ,
b'al'ma di v'ra chiruteih,

וְיַמְלִיךְ מַלְכוּתֵהּ,
v'yamlich malchuteih,

בְּחַיֵּיכוֹן וּבְיוֹמֵיכוֹן,
b'chayeichon uvyomeichon,

וּבְחַיֵּי דְכָל בֵּית יִשְׂרָאֵל
uvchayei d'chol beit Yisra·el

בַּעֲגָלָא וּבִזְמַן קָרִיב וְאִמְרוּ: אָמֵן.
ba·agala uvizman kariv, v'imru: **Amen.**

יְהֵא שְׁמֵהּ רַבָּא מְבָרַךְ
Y'hei sh'meih raba m'varach

לְעָלַם וּלְעָלְמֵי עָלְמַיָּא.
l'alam ulal'mei al'maya.

יִתְבָּרַךְ וְיִשְׁתַּבַּח וְיִתְפָּאַר
Yitbarach v'yishtabach v'yitpa·ar

וְיִתְרוֹמַם וְיִתְנַשֵּׂא וְיִתְהַדָּר
v'yit·romam v'yitnasei v'yit·hadar

וְיִתְעַלֶּה וְיִתְהַלָּל שְׁמֵהּ דְּקֻדְשָׁא
v'yitaleh v'yit·halal sh'meih d'kudsha

בְּרִיךְ הוּא,
brich Hu,

לְעֵלָּא
l'eila

During the Ten Days of Repentance:

וּלְעֵלָּא
uleila

מִן כָּל בִּרְכָתָא וְשִׁירָתָא
min kol birchata v'shirata,

תֻּשְׁבְּחָתָא וְנֶחֱמָתָא,
tushb'chata v'nechemata,

דַּאֲמִירָן בְּעָלְמָא,
da·amiran b'al'ma,

וְאִמְרוּ אָמֵן.
v'imru amen.

Magnified and sanctified! Magnified and sanctified!
May God's Great Name fill the world God created.
May God's splendor be seen in the world in your life, in your days,
in the life of all Israel. Quickly and soon! And let us say, Amen.
Forever may the Great Name be blessed!
Blessed and praised! Splendid and supreme!
May the holy Name, Bless God, be praised,

(During the Ten Days of Repentance: far,)

far beyond all the blessings and songs, comforts and consolations, that can be
offered in this world.
And let us say: Amen.

Psalm 23

מִזְמוֹר לְדָוִד,	Mizmor l'David.
יהוה רֹעִי, לֹא אֶחְסָר.	יהוה ro·i, lo echsar.
בִּנְאוֹת דֶּשֶׁא יַרְבִּיצֵנִי,	Binot desheh yarbitzeini,
עַל מֵי מְנֻחוֹת יְנַהֲלֵנִי.	al mei menuchot y'nahaleini.
נַפְשִׁי יְשׁוֹבֵב,	Nafshi y'shoveiv,
יַנְחֵנִי בְמַעְגְּלֵי צֶדֶק,	yancheini v'mag'lei tzedek,
לְמַעַן שְׁמוֹ.	lema·an sh'mo.
גַּם כִּי אֵלֵךְ בְּגֵיא צַלְמָוֶת,	Gam ki eilech b'gei tzalmavet,
לֹא אִירָא רָע כִּי אַתָּה עִמָּדִי,	lo ira ra, ki atah imadi,
שִׁבְטְךָ וּמִשְׁעַנְתֶּךָ,	shivt'cha umishantecha,
הֵמָּה יְנַחֲמֻנִי.	heimah y'nachamuni.
תַּעֲרֹךְ לְפָנַי, שֻׁלְחָן נֶגֶד צֹרְרָי,	Ta·aroch lefanai, shulchan neged tzor'rai,
דִּשַּׁנְתָּ בַשֶּׁמֶן רֹאשִׁי,	dishanta vashemen roshi
כּוֹסִי רְוָיָה.	kosi r'vayah.
אַךְ טוֹב וָחֶסֶד יִרְדְּפוּנִי	Ach tov vachesed yird'funi
כָּל יְמֵי חַיָּי,	kol y'mei chayai,
וְשַׁבְתִּי בְּבֵית יהוה	v'shavti b'veit יהוה
לְאֹרֶךְ יָמִים.	l'orech yamim.

A psalm of David:
יהוה is my shepherd; I shall not want.
God makes me lie down in green pastures
and leads me beside still waters to restore my soul;
God leads me in paths of righteousness
for the sake of God's name.
Though I walk through the valley
of the shadow of death,
I shall fear no evil,
for You are with me;
Your rod and Your staff, they comfort me.
You set a table before me
in the presence of my enemies.
You anoint my head with oil;
my cup overflows.
Truly goodness and mercy
will follow me
all the days of my life,
and I will dwell
in the house of יהוה forever.

My Constant Shepherd

The ETERNAL GOD is my constant shepherd;
I shall not lack for anything.
God brings me to rest in green pastures;
and leads me beside calming waters,
refreshing my soul; leading me in the winding paths of right action,
so that all will come to know God's ways.
Though I will walk through the valley of the shadow of death, may I fear no evil,
Knowing You are with me; Your callings and Your proddings are of comfort to me.
You prepare a table before me corresponding to my greatest challenges;
You call me to my most noble self; my life overflows with possibilities.
Surely goodness and kindness shall follow me all the days of my life,
and I will dwell in the House of the Sacred for the length of my days.

(Rabbi Eli Cohen)

מזמור לדוד   יהוה רעי לא אחסר
בנאות דשא ירביצני על מי מנוחות ינהלני
נפשי ישובב ינחני במעגלי צדק למען שמו
גם כי אלך   בגיא צלמות
לא אירא רע   כי אתה עמדי
שבטך ומשענתך   המה ינחמני
תערך לפני שלחן   נגד צררי
דשנת בשמן ראשי   כוסי רויה
אך טוב וחסד ירדפוני   כל ימי חיי
וישבתי בבית יהוה   לארך ימים

(safrut/calligraphy by Soferet Julie Seltzer)

El Malei Rachamim: God of Compassion

אֵל מָלֵא רַחֲמִים, שׁוֹכֵן בַּמְּרוֹמִים,
El malei rachamim, shochein bam'romim,

הַמְצֵא מְנוּחָה נְכוֹנָה
hamtzei m'nuchah n'chonah

תַּחַת כַּנְפֵי הַשְּׁכִינָה,
tachat kanfei hashechinah,

עִם קְדוֹשִׁים וּטְהוֹרִים
im k'doshim ut·horim

כְּזֹהַר הָרָקִיעַ מַזְהִירִים ,
k'zohar haraki·a maz·hirim ,

אֶת נִשְׁמַת _____
et nishmat _____

for a man say:

שֶׁהָלַךְ לְעוֹלָמוֹ
shehalach l'olamo,

בְּגַן עֵדֶן תְּהֵא מְנוּחָתוֹ.
b'gan Eden t'hei m'nucha·to.

אָנָּא בַּעַל הָרַחֲמִים יַסְתִּירֵהוּ
Ana ba·al harachamim yastirei·hu

בְּסֵתֶר כְּנָפֶיךָ לְעוֹלָמִים,
b'seiter k'nafecha l'olamim,

וְיִצְרֹר בִּצְרוֹר הַחַיִּים
v'yitzror bitzror hachayim

אֶת נִשְׁמָתוֹ, יהוה הוּא נַחֲלָתוֹ,
et nishmato. יהוה hu nachala·to.

וְיָנוּחַ בְּשָׁלוֹם עַל מִשְׁכָּבוֹ,
v'yanu·ach b'shalom al mishkavo,

וְנֹאמַר אָמֵן.
v'nomar amen.

for a woman say:

שֶׁהָלְכָה לְעוֹלָמָהּ
shehal'chah l'olamah,

בְּגַן עֵדֶן תְּהֵא מְנוּחָתָהּ.
b'gan Eden t'hei m'nucha·tah.

אָנָּא בַּעַל הָרַחֲמִים יַסְתִּירֶהָ
Ana ba·al harachamim yastirehah

בְּסֵתֶר כְּנָפֶיךָ לְעוֹלָמִים,
b'seiter k'nafecha l'olamim,

וְיִצְרֹר בִּצְרוֹר הַחַיִּים
v'yitzror bitzror hachayim

אֶת נִשְׁמָתָהּ, יהוה הוּא נַחֲלָתָהּ,
et nishmatah. יהוה hu nachalatah.

וְתָנוּחַ בְּשָׁלוֹם עַל מִשְׁכָּבָהּ,
v'tanu·ach b'shalom al mishkavah,

וְנֹאמַר אָמֵן.
v'nomar amen.

Compassionate God, Spirit of the universe,
Grant peace beneath the shelter of Your presence
among the holy and the pure
who shine with the splendor of the heavens,
to the soul of our dear one _____
who has gone to their reward.
May the Garden of Eden be their rest.
O God of mercy,
guard them forever in the shadow of Your wings.
May their soul be bound up in the bond of life.
May they rest in peace.
And let us say: Amen.

Elah M'lei·at Rachamim

This version of El Malei Rachamim uses feminine Hebrew,
speaking to divinity in feminine form.

אֱלָה מְלֵאַת רַחֲמִים Elah m'lei·at rachamim,

שׁוֹכֶנֶת בַּמְּרוֹמִים, shochenet bam'romim,

הַמְצִיאִי מְנוּחָה נְכוֹנָה hamtzi·i m'nuchah n'chonah

תַּחַת כַּנְפֵי הַשְּׁכִינָה tachat kanfei hashechinah

בְּמַעֲלוֹת קְדוֹשׁוֹת וּטְהוֹרוֹת b'ma·alot k'doshot ut·horot

כְּזֹהַר הָרָקִיעַ מַזְהִירוֹת k'zohar haraki·a maz·hirot

אֶת נִשְׁמַת _____ et nishmat _____

שֶׁהָלְכָה לְעוֹלָמָהּ shehal'cha l'olamah

בְּגַן עֵדֶן תְּהֵא מְנוּחָתָהּ. b'Gan Eden t'hei m'nuchatah.

אָנָּא גְּבִירַת הָרַחֲמִים Ana g'virat harachamim

תַּסְתִּירִיהָ בְּצֵל כְּנָפַיִךְ tastirihah betzel k'nafayich

לְעוֹלָמִים, וְצִרְרִי בִּצְרוֹר הַחַיִּים l'olamim, v'tzir'ri bitzror hachayim

אֶת נִשְׁמָתָהּ, et nishmatah,

שְׁכִינָה הִיא נַחֲלָתָהּ Shechinah hi nachalatah

וְתָנוּחַ בְּשָׁלוֹם עַל מִשְׁכָּבָהּ, v'tanu·ach b'shalom al mishkavah,

וְנֹאמַר: אָמֵן. v'nomar: Amen.

God filled with mercy,
dwelling in the heavens' heights,
bring proper rest
beneath the wings of your Shechinah,
amid the ranks of the holy and the pure
shining like the brilliance of the skies,
to the soul of our beloved _____
who has gone to her eternal place of rest.
May her rest be in the Garden of Eden.
May you who are the Source of Mercy
shelter her beneath your wings eternally,
and weave her soul into the web of life
that she may rest in peace.
And let us say: Amen.

(Rabbi Jill Hammer)

Aleinu

Short Aleinu I: Ein Od Mil'vado

אֵין עוֹד מִלְבַדּוֹ,   Ein od mil'vado,
יהוה הוּא הָאֱלֹהִים.   יהוה hu ha·elohim.

There is nothing but God.

Ein Od Mil'vado calligraphy by soferet Julie Seltzer.

Short Aleinu II: Vahasheivota

וַהֲשֵׁבֹתָ   Vahasheivota
אֶל לְבָבֶךְ   El levavecha
כִּי יהוה   Ki יהוה
הוּא הָאֱלֹהִים.   Hu ha·elohim.

And you will know in your heart
that God Who is Infinite is also God Who is close to us.

וְנֶאֱמַר: וְהָיָה יהוה   V'ne·emar: v'haya יהוה
לְמֶלֶךְ עַל כָּל הָאָרֶץ,   lemelech al kol ha·aretz,
בַּיּוֹם הַהוּא יִהְיֶה יהוה אֶחָד,   bayom hahu yihyeh יהוה echad
וּשְׁמוֹ אֶחָד.   ushmo echad.

And it is said: on that day יהוה will be God over all the earth,
and on that day יהוה will be One and God's Name will be One.

Aleinu (Full Text)

עָלֵינוּ לְשַׁבֵּחַ לַאֲדוֹן הַכֹּל,   Aleinu l'shabei·ach la·adon hakol,
לָתֵת גְּדֻלָּה לְיוֹצֵר בְּרֵאשִׁית,   lateit g'dulah l'yotzeir b'reishit,
שֶׁלֹּא/שֶׁלּוֹ*   shelo
עָשָׂנוּ כְּגוֹיֵי הָאֲרָצוֹת,   asanu k'goyei ha·aratzot,
וְלֹא/וְלוֹ*   v'lo
שָׂמָנוּ כְּמִשְׁפְּחוֹת הָאֲדָמָה,   samanu k'mishp'chot ha·adamah,
שֶׁלֹּא/שֶׁלּוֹ*   shelo
שָׂם חֶלְקֵנוּ כָּהֶם,   sam chelkeinu kahem,
וְגֹרָלֵנוּ כְּכָל הֲמוֹנָם.   v'goraleinu k'chol hamonam.

It is up to us to praise the Source of all, to exalt the Molder of creation.
We are:

made for God	(or)	not made like
like all nations.		other nations.

We are:

placed here for God	(or)	unlike
like all humanity.		other peoples.

Our portion and our fate are:

for God's	(or)	not like those
own sake.		of other peoples.

וַאֲנַחְנוּ כּוֹרְעִים   Va·anachnu kor'im
וּמִשְׁתַּחֲוִים וּמוֹדִים,   umishtachavim umodim,
לִפְנֵי מֶלֶךְ,   lifnei melech
מַלְכֵי הַמְּלָכִים,   malchei ham'lachim,
הַקָּדוֹשׁ בָּרוּךְ הוּא.   hakadosh baruch hu.

We bow low and prostrate in thanks
before the Source of all sources,
the Holy One, blessed is God.

---

* Pray either לֹא, pronounced Lo ("not"), or לוֹ, also pronounced Lo ("for God").
The first articulates Jewish chosenness; the second, post-triumphalism.

שֶׁהוּא נוֹטֶה שָׁמַיִם וְיֹסֵד אָרֶץ,
Shehu noteh shamayim v'yoseid aretz,

וּמוֹשַׁב יְקָרוֹ בַּשָּׁמַיִם מִמַּעַל,
umoshav y'karo bashamayim mima·al,

וּשְׁכִינַת עֻזּוֹ בְּגָבְהֵי מְרוֹמִים.
ush·chinat uzo b'govhei m'romim.

הוּא אֱלֹהֵינוּ, אֵין עוֹד.
Hu Eloheinu, ein od.

God sets out the heavens and establishes the earth.
God's honored place is in the heights of our aspirations;
God's powerful presence is in the heavens of our hopes.
This is our God; there is none else.

אֱמֶת מַלְכֵּנוּ אֶפֶס זוּלָתוֹ.
Emet malkeinu efes zulato.

כַּכָּתוּב בְּתוֹרָתוֹ: וְיָדַעְתָּ הַיּוֹם
Kakatuv b'torato: V'yadata hayom

וַהֲשֵׁבֹתָ אֶל לְבָבֶךָ,
vahasheivota el l'vavecha,

כִּי יהוה הוּא הָאֱלֹהִים בַּשָּׁמַיִם
ki יהוה hu ha·elohim bashamayim

מִמַּעַל, וְעַל הָאָרֶץ מִתָּחַת, אֵין עוֹד.
mima·al, v'al ha·aretz mitachat, ein od.

There is nothing that God is not.
As it is written in God's sacred teaching:
"You shall know this day
and place upon your heart
that יהוה is God in heaven above and earth below;
there is none else."

עַל כֵּן נְקַוֶּה לְךָ יהוה אֱלֹהֵינוּ,
Al kein n'kaveh l'cha יהוה Eloheinu,

לִרְאוֹת מְהֵרָה בְּתִפְאֶרֶת עֻזֶּךָ,
lirot m'heirah b'tiferet uzecha,

לְהַעֲבִיר גִּלּוּלִים מִן הָאָרֶץ
l'ha·avir gilulim min ha·aretz,

וְהָאֱלִילִים כָּרוֹת יִכָּרֵתוּן,
v'ha·elilim karot yikareitun,

לְתַקֵּן עוֹלָם בְּמַלְכוּת שַׁדַּי.
l'takein olam b'malchut Shaddai.

וְכָל בְּנֵי בָשָׂר יִקְרְאוּ בִשְׁמֶךָ,
V'chol b'nei vasar yikr'u vishmecha,

לְהַפְנוֹת אֵלֶיךָ כָּל רִשְׁעֵי אָרֶץ.
l'hafnot eilecha kol rishei aretz.

יַכִּירוּ וְיֵדְעוּ כָּל יוֹשְׁבֵי תֵבֵל,
Yakiru v'yeid'u kol yosh'vei teiveil

כִּי לְךָ תִּכְרַע כָּל בֶּרֶךְ
ki l'cha tichra kol berech

תִּשָּׁבַע כָּל לָשׁוֹן.
tishava kol lashon.

Therefore we hope in You, יהוה our God. May we soon see the power of
Your beauty wipe away false gods from the earth and sweep away idolatry,
so that the truth of Your sovereign presence will repair the world.
Then will all humanity call Your name,
and then all that had been dark will turn to Your light.
All who dwell on earth will feel in their hearts and know in their minds
that You are our source—the true object of devotion and loyalty.

לְפָנֶיךָ יהוה אֱלֹהֵינוּ יִכְרְעוּ וְיִפֹּלוּ, L'fanecha יהוה Eloheinu yichr'u v'yipolu,

וְלִכְבוֹד שִׁמְךָ יְקָר יִתֵּנוּ. v'lichvod shimcha y'kar yiteinu.

וִיקַבְּלוּ כֻלָּם אֶת עוֹל מַלְכוּתֶךָ. Vikab'lu chulam et ol malchutecha.

וְתִמְלֹךְ עֲלֵיהֶם מְהֵרָה לְעוֹלָם וָעֶד. V'timloch aleihem m'heirah l'olam va·ed.

כִּי הַמַּלְכוּת שֶׁלְּךָ הִיא, Ki hamalchut shel'cha hi,

וּלְעוֹלְמֵי עַד תִּמְלוֹךְ בְּכָבוֹד. ulol'mei ad timloch b'chavod.

Before You, יהוה our God, will they bend low
and pay homage to glorify Your name.
Then all will accept the obligations of living in Your world—
obligations of hope, love and duty to heaven and humanity.
Then You will surely rule forever and ever.
For the earth is Yours, and Your glory fills it forever.

כַּכָּתוּב בְּתוֹרָתֶךָ: Kakatuv b'toratecha:

יהוה יִמְלֹךְ לְעוֹלָם וָעֶד. יהוה yimloch l'olam va·ed.

וְנֶאֱמַר: V'ne·emar:

וְהָיָה יהוה לְמֶלֶךְ v'hayah יהוה lemelech

עַל כָּל הָאָרֶץ, al kol ha·aretz,

בַּיוֹם הַהוּא יִהְיֶה יהוה אֶחָד, bayom hahu yihyeh יהוה echad,

וּשְׁמוֹ אֶחָד. ushmo echad.

Then shall your realm be established on earth,
and the word of Your prophet fulfilled:
"יהוה will reign forever and ever.
On that day, יהוה shall be One, and God's name shall be One."

Mourner's Kaddish

יִתְגַּדַּל וְיִתְקַדַּשׁ שְׁמֵהּ רַבָּא, — Yitgadal v'yitkadash, sh'meih raba,

בְּעָלְמָא דִּי בְרָא כִרְעוּתֵהּ, — b'al'ma di v'ra chiruteih,

וְיַמְלִיךְ מַלְכוּתֵהּ — v'yamlich malchuteih

בְּחַיֵּיכוֹן וּבְיוֹמֵיכוֹן — b'chayeichon uvyomeichon

וּבְחַיֵּי דְכָל בֵּית יִשְׂרָאֵל, — uvchayei d'chol beit Yisra·el,

בַּעֲגָלָא וּבִזְמַן קָרִיב, — ba·agala uvizman kariv,

וְאִמְרוּ: אָמֵן. — v'imru: **Amen.**

יְהֵא שְׁמֵהּ רַבָּא מְבָרַךְ — Y'hei sh'mei raba m'varach

לְעָלַם וּלְעָלְמֵי עָלְמַיָּא. — l'alam ulal'mei al'maya.

יִתְבָּרַךְ וְיִשְׁתַּבַּח, וְיִתְפָּאַר — Yitbarach v'yishtabach v'yitpa·ar

וְיִתְרוֹמַם וְיִתְנַשֵּׂא וְיִתְהַדָּר וְיִתְעַלֶּה — v'yit·romam v'yitnasei v'yit·hadar v'yitaleh

וְיִתְהַלָּל שְׁמֵהּ דְּקֻדְשָׁא — v'yit·halal sh'meih d'kudsha

בְּרִיךְ הוּא — **b'rich hu**

לְעֵלָּא — l'eila

During the Ten Days of Repentance:

וּלְעֵלָּא — uleila

מִן כָּל בִּרְכָתָא וְשִׁירָתָא, — min kol birchata v'shirata,

תֻּשְׁבְּחָתָא וְנֶחֱמָתָא, — tushb'chata v'nechemata,

דַּאֲמִירָן בְּעָלְמָא, וְאִמְרוּ: אָמֵן. — da·amiran b'al'ma, v'imru: Amen.

יְהֵא שְׁלָמָא רַבָּא מִן שְׁמַיָּא — Y'hei sh'lama raba min sh'maya

וְחַיִּים עָלֵינוּ וְעַל כָּל יִשְׂרָאֵל, — v'chayim aleinu v'al kol Yisra·el,

וְאִמְרוּ: אָמֵן. — v'imru: Amen.

עֹשֶׂה שָׁלוֹם בִּמְרוֹמָיו — Oseh shalom bimromav,

הוּא יַעֲשֶׂה שָׁלוֹם עָלֵינוּ — hu ya·aseh shalom, aleinu

וְעַל כָּל יִשְׂרָאֵל, — v'al kol Yisra·el,

וְעַל כָּל יוֹשְׁבֵי תֵבֵל, — v'al kol yosh'vei teiveil,

וְאִמְרוּ: אָמֵן. — v'imru: **Amen.**

Mourner's Kaddish

The Great Essence will flower in our lives
And expand throughout the world.
May we learn to let it shine through so we can augment its glory.
We praise, we continue to praise,
And yet, whatever it is we praise, is quite beyond the grasp
Of all the words and symbols that point us toward it.
We know, yet we do not know.
May great peace pour forth from the heavens for us,
For all Israel, and for all who struggle toward truth.
May that which makes harmony in the cosmos above,
Bring peace within and between us, and to all who dwell on this earth.
May the Source of peace send peace to all who mourn
And comfort all who are bereaved.

(translation: Rabbi Burt Jacobson)

(Each time Mourner's Kaddish appears in this volume, it is translated by someone different. Each translation is unique, and each evokes a particular quality of the original Aramaic.)

Magnified and Sanctified

The process of dying is painful
Especially if it is prolonged
But death itself is a transition
A transfer from here to there
A recycling of the body and the soul.
Matter is never destroyed, only transformed
So too does the soul evolve,
Higher and higher
From instinct to inspiration,
From haughtiness to holiness
From selfishness to service,
From individualism to union,
Until it returns home to the Soul of Souls
The *Ein Sof*, the infinite one.
This is the Divine Source of Life,
Magnified and sanctified.

(Rabbi Allen Maller)

Maariv / Evening Prayer

Lighting the *Shiva* Candle for the First Time

May the light of this candle gleam like the soul of _____.

May the light of this candle bring me comfort and keep me company.

And, when this candle is gone, may the memory of _____ continue to illuminate my days.

יהוה יהוה אוֹרִי וְיִשְׁעִי, מִמִּי אִירָא? ori v'yishi; mimi ira?

יהוה יהוה מָעוֹז חַיַּי, מִמִּי אֶפְחָד? maoz chayai, mimi efchad?

If יהוה is my light and my redemption, what shall I fear?
If יהוה is the strength of my life, what shall make me afraid? (Psalm 27:1)

שְׁמַע יִשְׂרָאֵל, Sh'ma Yisra·el,

יהוה אֱלֹהֵינוּ, יהוה אֶחָד. יהוה Eloheinu, יהוה echad.

Hear, O Israel; יהוה is our God; יהוה is One.

The Sh'ma and Her Blessings

Bar'chu — Call to Prayer

As we bless the Source of Life, so we are blessed.
And the blessing gives us strength, and makes our visions clear;
And the blessing gives us peace, and the courage to dare.
As we bless the Source of Life, so we are blessed.

(Faith Rogow)

V'Hu Rachum / The Merciful One

וְהוּא רַחוּם יְכַפֵּר עָוֹן וְלֹא יַשְׁחִית,   V'Hu rachum y'chapeir avon v'lo yash·chit,
וְהִרְבָּה לְהָשִׁיב אַפּוֹ,   v'hirbah l'hashiv apo,
וְלֹא יָעִיר כָּל חֲמָתוֹ.   v'lo ya·ir kol chamato.
יהוה, הוֹשִׁיעָה, הַמֶּלֶךְ יַעֲנֵנוּ   יהוה, hoshi·a, hamelech ya·aneinu
בְיוֹם קָרְאֵנוּ.   v'yom koreinu.

The Merciful One will cover iniquity and not forever destroy.
Soon may God withdraw anger;
may divine rage not be aroused.
יהוה, save us, You who answer
on the day when we call.

Bar'chu, Dear One

Bar'chu, Dear One—Shechinah, holy Name
As I call on the light of my soul I come home.

(Rabbi Lev Friedman)

בָּרְכוּ אֶת יהוה הַמְבֹרָךְ.   Bar'chu et יהוה hamvorach.

בָּרוּךְ יהוה הַמְבֹרָךְ לְעוֹלָם וָעֶד.   Baruch יהוה hamvorach l'olam va·ed.

Blessed is יהוה, the blessed One.

Blessed is יהוה, the blessed One, now and forever!

Ma·ariv Aravim / Who Evens the Evenings

בָּרוּךְ אַתָּה, יהוה,   Baruch atah, יהוה,

אֱלֹהֵינוּ מֶלֶךְ הָעוֹלָם,   Eloheinu, melech ha·olam,

אֲשֶׁר בִּדְבָרוֹ מַעֲרִיב עֲרָבִים,   asher bidvaro ma·ariv aravim,

בְּחָכְמָה פּוֹתֵחַ שְׁעָרִים,   b'chochmah potei·ach sh'arim,

וּבִתְבוּנָה מְשַׁנֶּה עִתִּים,   uvitvunah m'shaneh itim,

וּמַחֲלִיף אֶת הַזְּמַנִּים,   umachalif et haz'manim,

וּמְסַדֵּר אֶת הַכּוֹכָבִים   umsadeir et hakochavim

בְּמִשְׁמְרוֹתֵיהֶם בָּרָקִיעַ כִּרְצוֹנוֹ.   b'mishm'roteihem baraki·a kirtzono.

בּוֹרֵא יוֹם וָלָיְלָה,   Borei yom valailah,

גּוֹלֵל אוֹר מִפְּנֵי חֹשֶׁךְ,   goleil or mip'nei choshech

וְחֹשֶׁךְ מִפְּנֵי אוֹר.   v'choshech mip'nei or.

וּמַעֲבִיר יוֹם וּמֵבִיא לָיְלָה,   Uma·avir yom umeivi lailah,

וּמַבְדִּיל בֵּין יוֹם וּבֵין לָיְלָה,   umavdil bein yom uvein lailah,

יהוה צְבָאוֹת שְׁמוֹ.   יהוה Tz'vaot sh'mo.

אֵל חַי וְקַיָּם,   El chai v'kayam,

תָּמִיד יִמְלוֹךְ עָלֵינוּ לְעוֹלָם וָעֶד.   tamid yimloch aleinu l'olam va·ed.

בָּרוּךְ אַתָּה, יהוה,   Baruch atah, יהוה,

הַמַּעֲרִיב עֲרָבִים.   hama·ariv aravim.

Blessed are You, יהוה our God, Source of all being,
by Whose word the evening falls.
In wisdom You open heaven's gates.
With understanding You make seasons change,
causing the times to come and go,
and ordering the stars on their appointed paths
through heaven's dome, all according to Your will.
Creator of day and night, who rolls back light before dark,
and dark before light, who makes day pass away
and brings on the night, dividing between day and night;
the Leader of Heaven's Multitudes is Your name!
Living and enduring God, be our guide now and always.
Blessed are You, Source of All being,
Who makes evening fall.

Evening

You mix the watercolors of the evening
like my son, swishing his brush
until the waters are black with paint.
The sky is streaked and dimming.

The sun wheels over the horizon
like a glowing penny falling into its slot.
Day is spent, and in its place: the changing moon,
the spatterdash of stars across the sky's expanse.

Every evening we tell ourselves the old story:
You cover over our sins, forgiveness
like a fleece blanket tucked around our ears.
When we cry out, You will hear.

Soothe my fear of life without enough light.
Rock me to sleep in the deepening dark.

                                        (Rabbi Rachel Barenblat)

Ahavat Olam / Unending Love

אַהֲבַת עוֹלָם Ahavat olam
בֵּית יִשְׂרָאֵל עַמְּךָ אָהָבְתָּ, beit Yisra·el am'cha ahavta
תּוֹרָה וּמִצְוֹת, חֻקִּים וּמִשְׁפָּטִים Torah umitzvot chukim umishpatim
אוֹתָנוּ לִמַּדְתָּ. otanu limadta.
עַל כֵּן, יהוה, אֱלֹהֵינוּ, Al kein, יהוה, Eloheinu,
בְּשָׁכְבֵנוּ וּבְקוּמֵנוּ b'shochveinu uvkumeinu
נָשִׂיחַ בְּחֻקֶּיךָ, וְנִשְׂמַח בְּדִבְרֵי nasi·ach b'chukecha, v'nismach b'divrei
תוֹרָתֶךָ וּבְמִצְוֹתֶיךָ toratecha uvmitzvotecha
לְעוֹלָם וָעֶד. l'olam va·ed.
כִּי הֵם חַיֵּינוּ וְאֹרֶךְ יָמֵינוּ, Ki heim chayeinu v'orech yameinu,
וּבָהֶם נֶהְגֶּה יוֹמָם וָלָיְלָה. uvahem nehgeh yomam valailah.

וְאַהֲבָתְךָ V'ahavat'cha
אַל תָּסִיר מִמֶּנּוּ לְעוֹלָמִים. al tasir mimenu l'olamim.
בָּרוּךְ אַתָּה, יהוה, Baruch atah, יהוה,
אוֹהֵב עַמּוֹ יִשְׂרָאֵל. oheiv amo Yisra·el.

With eternal love,
You love the house of Israel.
Torah and mitzvot, laws and justice
You have taught us.
And so, יהוה, our God,
when we lie down and when we rise,
we reflect upon Your laws; we take pleasure
in Your Torah's words and your mitzvot,
now and always.
Truly, they are our life, our length of days.
On them we meditate by day and night.

Your love
will never depart from us as long as worlds endure.
Blessed are You, יהוה,
who loves Your people Israel.

Unending Love

We are loved by unending love.

We are embraced by arms that find us
even when we are hidden from ourselves.
We are touched by fingers that soothe us
even when we are too proud for soothing.
We are counseled by voices that guide us
even when we are too embittered to hear.

We are loved by unending love.

We are supported by hands that uplift us
even in the midst of a fall.
We are urged on by eyes that meet us
even when we are too weak for meeting.

We are loved by unending love.

Embraced, touched, soothed, and counseled,
ours are the arms, the fingers, the voices;
ours are the hands, the eyes, the smiles;

We are loved by unending love.

(Rabbi Rami Shapiro)

Sh'ma / Oneness

שְׁמַע יִשְׂרָאֵל,   **Sh'ma Yisra·el:**
יהוה אֱלֹהֵינוּ, יהוה אֶחָד!   יהוה **Eloheinu** יהוה **echad!**

בָּרוּךְ שֵׁם כְּבוֹד מַלְכוּתוֹ   (Baruch shem k'vod malchuto
לְעוֹלָם וָעֶד.   l'olam va·ed.)

Hear, O Israel:
יהוה is our God, יהוה is One!
(Through time and space Your glory shines, Majestic One!)

וְאָהַבְתָּ אֵת יהוה אֱלֹהֶיךָ,   V'ahavta et יהוה Elohecha,
בְּכָל לְבָבְךָ,וּבְכָל נַפְשְׁךָ,   b'chol levav'cha, uvchol nafsh'cha,
וּבְכָל מְאֹדֶךָ.   uvchol-m'odecha.
וְהָיוּ הַדְּבָרִים הָאֵלֶּה, אֲשֶׁר אָנֹכִי   V'hayu had'varim ha·eileh, asher anochi
מְצַוְּךָ הַיּוֹם, עַל לְבָבֶךָ.   m'tzav'cha hayom, al l'vavecha.
וְשִׁנַּנְתָּם לְבָנֶיךָ, וְדִבַּרְתָּ בָּם,   V'shinantam l'vanecha, v'dibarta bam,
בְּשִׁבְתְּךָ בְּבֵיתֶךָ, וּבְלֶכְתְּךָ בַדֶּרֶךְ,   b'shivt'cha b'veitecha, uvlecht'cha vaderech,
וּבְשָׁכְבְּךָ, וּבְקוּמֶךָ.   uvshochb'cha, uvkumecha.
וּקְשַׁרְתָּם לְאוֹת עַל יָדֶךָ,   Ukshartam l'ot al yadecha,
וְהָיוּ לְטֹטָפֹת בֵּין עֵינֶיךָ.   v'hayu l'totafot bein einecha.
וּכְתַבְתָּם   Uchtavtam
עַל מְזֻזוֹת בֵּיתֶךָ וּבִשְׁעָרֶיךָ.   al m'zuzot beitecha uvisharecha.

Love the One, your God,
with every heartbeat, with every breath,
with every conscious act.
Keep in mind the words
I command you today.
Teach them to your children, talk about them at work;
whether you are tired or you are rested.
Let them guide the work of your hands;
keep them in the forefront of your vision.
Do not leave them at the doorway, or outside your gate.

וְהָיָה אִם שָׁמֹעַ תִּשְׁמְעוּ
V'hayah im shamo·a tishm'u

אֶל מִצְוֹתַי, אֲשֶׁר אָנֹכִי מְצַוֶּה
el-mitzvotai, asher anochi m'tzaveh

אֶתְכֶם הַיּוֹם,
etchem hayom,

לְאַהֲבָה אֶת יהוה אֱלֹהֵיכֶם
l'ahavah et יהוה Eloheichem

וּלְעָבְדוֹ, בְּכָל לְבַבְכֶם
ulovdo, b'chol levavchem

וּבְכָל נַפְשְׁכֶם.
uvchol nafsh'chem.

וְנָתַתִּי מְטַר אַרְצְכֶם בְּעִתּוֹ,
V'natati m'tar-artz'chem b'ito,

יוֹרֶה וּמַלְקוֹשׁ, וְאָסַפְתָּ דְגָנֶךָ
yoreh umalkosh, v'asafta d'ganecha

וְתִירֹשְׁךָ וְיִצְהָרֶךָ.
v'tirosh'cha v'yitz·harecha.

וְנָתַתִּי עֵשֶׂב בְּשָׂדְךָ לִבְהֶמְתֶּךָ,
v'natati eisev b'sad'cha livhemtecha,

וְאָכַלְתָּ וְשָׂבָעְתָּ.
v'achalta v'savata.

הִשָּׁמְרוּ לָכֶם פֶּן יִפְתֶּה לְבַבְכֶם,
Hisham'ru lachem pen yifteh l'vavchem,

וְסַרְתֶּם וַעֲבַדְתֶּם אֱלֹהִים אֲחֵרִים
v'sartem va'avadtem elohim acheirim

וְהִשְׁתַּחֲוִיתֶם לָהֶם.
v'hishtachavitem lahem.

וְחָרָה אַף יהוה בָּכֶם,
V'charah af יהוה bachem,

וְעָצַר אֶת הַשָּׁמַיִם
v'atzar et hashamayim

וְלֹא יִהְיֶה מָטָר,
v'lo yihyeh matar,

וְהָאֲדָמָה לֹא תִתֵּן אֶת יְבוּלָהּ,
v'ha·adamah lo titen et y'vulah,

וַאֲבַדְתֶּם מְהֵרָה מֵעַל הָאָרֶץ הַטֹּבָה
va'avadtem m'heirah mei·al ha·aretz hatovah

אֲשֶׁר יהוה נֹתֵן לָכֶם.
asher יהוה notein lachem.

וְשַׂמְתֶּם אֶת דְּבָרַי אֵלֶּה
V'samtem et d'varai eileh

עַל לְבַבְכֶם וְעַל נַפְשְׁכֶם,
al levavchem v'al nafsh'chem,

וּקְשַׁרְתֶּם אֹתָם לְאוֹת עַל יֶדְכֶם,
ukshartem otam l'ot al yedchem,

וְהָיוּ לְטוֹטָפֹת בֵּין עֵינֵיכֶם.
v'hayu l'totafot bein eineichem.

וְלִמַּדְתֶּם אֹתָם אֶת בְּנֵיכֶם
V'limadtem otam et b'neichem

לְדַבֵּר בָּם, בְּשִׁבְתְּךָ בְּבֵיתֶךָ,
ledabeir bam, b'shivt'cha b'veitecha,

וּבְלֶכְתְּךָ בַדֶּרֶךְ,
uvlecht'cha vaderech,

וּבְשָׁכְבְּךָ, וּבְקוּמֶךָ.
uvshochb'cha uv'kumecha.

וּכְתַבְתָּם עַל מְזוּזוֹת בֵּיתֶךָ
Uchtavtam al m'zuzot beitecha

וּבִשְׁעָרֶיךָ.
uvisharecha.

לְמַעַן יִרְבּוּ יְמֵיכֶם וִימֵי בְנֵיכֶם
Lema·an yirbu y'meichem vimei v'neichem

עַל הָאֲדָמָה אֲשֶׁר נִשְׁבַּע יהוה
al ha·adamah asher nishba יהוה

לַאֲבֹתֵיכֶם לָתֵת לָהֶם,
la·avoteichem lateit lahem,

כִּימֵי הַשָּׁמַיִם עַל הָאָרֶץ.
kimei hashamayim al ha·aretz.

How good it will be when you really listen
and hear My directions
which I give you today,
to love יהוה, who is your God,
and to act godly with feeling and inspiration.
Your earthly needs will be met at the right time,
appropriate to the season.
You will reap what you have planted
for your delight and health.
Also your animals will have ample feed.
All of you will eat and be content.

Be careful—watch out!
Don't let your cravings delude you;
don't become alienated;
don't let your cravings become your gods;
don't debase yourself to them
because the God-sense within you
will become distorted.
Heaven will be shut to you,
grace will not descend,
Earth will not yield her produce.
Your rushing will destroy you!
And Earth will not be able to recover
her good balance
in which God's gifts manifest.

(translation: Rabbi Zalman Schachter-Shalomi z"l)

Listen Up Y'all / An interpretive version of וְהָיָה אִם שָׁמֹעַ

"Listen up, y'all," says Shekhinah
who looks today like a teacher
in corduroy dress and sedate boots.

"Let the smartphone rest a bit,
or learn how to hear My voice
coming through its speaker.

Let your love for Me well up
like unexpected tears. Everyone serves
something: give your life to Me.

Let the channel of your heart open
and My abundance will pour through.
But if you prefer profit, if you pretend —

if you're not real with Me —
your life will feel hollow
and your heart be embittered.

I won't punish you; I won't need to.
Your hollowness will be punishment enough,
and the world will suffer for it.

So let My words twine around your arm,
and shine like a headlamp
between your eyes to light your way.

Teach them to everyone you meet.
Write them at the end of your emails
and on your business cards.

Then you'll remember how to live
with the flow of all that is holy —
you'll have heaven right here on earth.

(Rabbi Rachel Barenblat)

וַיֹּאמֶר יהוה אֶל מֹשֶׁה לֵּאמֹר. Vayomer יהוה el Mosheh leimor.
דַּבֵּר אֶל בְּנֵי יִשְׂרָאֵל וְאָמַרְתָּ אֲלֵהֶם, Dabeir el b'nei Yisra-el v'amarta aleihem,
וְעָשׂוּ לָהֶם צִיצִת עַל כַּנְפֵי בִגְדֵיהֶם v'asu lahem tzitzit al kanfei vigdeihem
לְדֹרֹתָם, וְנָתְנוּ עַל צִיצִת הַכָּנָף ledorotam, v'nat'nu al tzitzit hakanaf
פְּתִיל תְּכֵלֶת. וְהָיָה לָכֶם לְצִיצִת, p'til t'cheilet. V'yahah lachem l'tzitzit,
וּרְאִיתֶם אֹתוֹ uritem oto,
וּזְכַרְתֶּם אֶת כָּל מִצְוֺת יהוה, uzchartem et kol mitzvot יהוה
וַעֲשִׂיתֶם אֹתָם, va-asitem otam.
וְלֹא תָתֻוּרוּ אַחֲרֵי לְבַבְכֶם V'lo taturu acharei l'vavchem
וְאַחֲרֵי עֵינֵיכֶם, v'acharei eineichem,
אֲשֶׁר אַתֶּם זֹנִים אַחֲרֵיהֶם. asher atem zonim achareihem.
לְמַעַן תִּזְכְּרוּ וַעֲשִׂיתֶם Lema-an tizk'ru va'asitem
אֶת כָּל מִצְוֺתָי, et kol mitzvotai,
וִהְיִיתֶם קְדֹשִׁים לֵאלֹהֵיכֶם. vihyitem k'doshim leiloheichem
אֲנִי יהוה אֱלֹהֵיכֶם, Ani יהוה Eloheichem,
אֲשֶׁר הוֹצֵאתִי אֶתְכֶם מֵאֶרֶץ מִצְרַיִם, asher hotzeiti et-chem mei-eretz Mitzrayim,
לִהְיוֹת לָכֶם לֵאלֹהִים, lihyot lachem leilohim;
אֲנִי יהוה אֱלֹהֵיכֶם. ani יהוה Eloheichem.

יהוה Who Is said to Moshe:
Speak, telling the Yisra·el folks to make tzitzit
on the corners of their garments,
so they will have generations to follow them.
On each tzitzit-tassel let them set a blue thread.
Glance at it, and, in your seeing,
remember all of the other directives of יהוה who Is, and act on them!
This way you will not be led astray, craving to see and want,
and then prostitute yourself for your cravings.
This way you will be mindful to actualize my directions
for becoming dedicated to your God,
to be aware that I AM יהוה who is your God —
the One who freed you from the oppression in order to God you.
I am יהוה your God.
This way you will be mindful to actualize my directions
for becoming dedicated to your God;
to be aware that I am your God,
the one who freed you from the oppression
in order to be your God. I am Adonai your God.
That is the truth!

(translation: Rabbi Zalman Schachter-Shalomi z"l)

Ge'ulah / Redemption

אֱמֶת וֶאֱמוּנָה כָּל זֹאת,
Emet ve·emunah kol zot,

וְקַיָּם עָלֵינוּ, כִּי הוּא
v'kayam aleinu, ki Hu

יהוה אֱלֹהֵינוּ וְאֵין זוּלָתוֹ,
יהוה Eloheinu v'ein zulato,

וַאֲנַחְנוּ יִשְׂרָאֵל עַמּוֹ.
va·anachnu Yisra·el amo.

הַפּוֹדֵנוּ מִיַּד מְלָכִים,
Hapodeinu miyad m'lachim,

מַלְכֵּנוּ הַגּוֹאֲלֵנוּ מִכַּף
Malkeinu hago·aleinu mikaf

כָּל הֶעָרִיצִים.
kol he·aritzim.

הָאֵל הַנִּפְרָע לָנוּ מִצָּרֵינוּ,
Ha·El hanifra lanu mitzareinu,

וְהַמְשַׁלֵּם גְּמוּל לְכָל אֹיְבֵי נַפְשֵׁנוּ,
v'ham'shaleim g'mul l'chol oy'vei nafsheinu,

הָעֹשֶׂה גְדוֹלוֹת עַד אֵין חֵקֶר,
ha·oseh g'dolot ad ein cheiker,

נִסִּים וְנִפְלָאוֹת עַד אֵין מִסְפָּר.
nisim v'nifla·ot ad ein mispar.

הַשָּׂם נַפְשֵׁנוּ בַּחַיִּים,
Hasam nafsheinu bachayim,

וְלֹא נָתַן לַמּוֹט רַגְלֵנוּ,
v'lo natan lamot ragleinu,

הַמַּדְרִיכֵנוּ עַל בָּמוֹת אוֹיְבֵינוּ,
hamadricheinu al bamot oy'veinu,

וַיָּרֶם קַרְנֵנוּ עַל כָּל שׂוֹנְאֵינוּ.
vayarem karneinu al kol son'einu.

הָעֹשֶׂה לָנוּ נִסִּים וּנְקָמָה בְּפַרְעֹה,
Ha·oseh lanu nisim unkamah b'Faroh,

אוֹתוֹת וּמוֹפְתִים בְּאַדְמַת בְּנֵי חָם
otot umof'tim b'admat b'nei cham,

וַיּוֹצֵא אֶת עַמּוֹ יִשְׂרָאֵל מִתּוֹכָם
vayotzei et amo Yisra·el mitocham

לְחֵרוּת עוֹלָם.
l'cheirut olam.

הַמַּעֲבִיר בָּנָיו בֵּין גִּזְרֵי יַם סוּף,
Hama·avir banav bein gizrei yam suf,

וְרָאוּ בָנָיו גְּבוּרָתוֹ,
v'ra·u vanav g'vurato,

שִׁבְּחוּ וְהוֹדוּ לִשְׁמוֹ.
shib'chu v'hodu lishmo.

וּמַלְכוּתוֹ בְּרָצוֹן קִבְּלוּ עֲלֵיהֶם,
U'malchuto b'ratzon kib'lu aleihem,

מֹשֶׁה וּמִרְיָם וּבְנֵי יִשְׂרָאֵל
Mosheh uMiryam uvnei Yisra·el

לְךָ עָנוּ שִׁירָה בְּשִׂמְחָה רַבָּה,
l'cha anu shirah b'simchah raba,

וְאָמְרוּ כֻלָּם:
v'am'ru chulam:

True and enduring, right and real, are these truths:
that You, יהוה, are our God and there is none like You,
and we, Israel / the God-wrestlers, are Your people.

You rescue us from the hands of kings and sovereigns.
You are the God Who brought us forth from the Narrow Place
and rescued us from the enemies of our souls.
You are the One Who does great wonders and miracles beyond counting.
You redeem us into life and do not give us over into death.
You lead us away from places and people of enmity toward us.

You did signs and wonders for us before Pharaoh.
Your might led to the death of the first-borns of Egypt
as you led Your people Israel into freedom.
You led us through the Sea of Reeds,
and, as everyone saw Your might,
we sang grateful praises to Your name.

Perceiving and accepting Your sovereignty,
Moshe, Miryam, and all Israel sang this song
to you in great joy, and together they said:

מִי כָמֹכָה בָּאֵלִם יהוה,   Mi chamocha ba·eilim, יהוה?
מִי כָּמֹכָה נֶאְדָּר בַּקֹּדֶשׁ,   Mi kamocha nedar bakodesh,
נוֹרָא תְהִלֹּת, עֹשֵׂה פֶלֶא.   nora t'hilot, oseih feleh.

מַלְכוּתְךָ רָאוּ בָנֶיךָ,   Malchut'cha ra·u vanecha,
בּוֹקֵעַ יָם לִפְנֵי מֹשֶׁה וּמִרְיָם,   bokei·a yam lifnei Mosheh uMiryam.
זֶה אֵלִי עָנוּ וְאָמְרוּ:   Zeh Eili anu v'am'ru
יהוה יִמְלֹךְ לְעוֹלָם וָעֶד.   יהוה yimloch l'olam va·ed!

וְנֶאֱמַר: כִּי פָדָה יהוה אֶת יַעֲקֹב,   V'ne·emar: Ki fadah יהוה et Ya·akov;
וּגְאָלוֹ מִיַּד חָזָק מִמֶּנּוּ.   ugalo miyad chazak mimenu.
בָּרוּךְ אַתָּה, יהוה, גָּאַל יִשְׂרָאֵל.   Baruch atah, יהוה, ga·al Yisra·el.

Who is like You, among the gods, יהוה?
Who is like You, awesome and doing wonders?
Your children saw your majesty,
splitting the sea before Moses and Miryam.
"This is our God," they cried,
"יהוה will reign through all space and time!"
And it is said:
יהוה has saved the people of Jacob
and redeems the weak from the mighty.
Blessed are You, יהוה, who redeems Israel.

Journey

between
a pillar of cloud
and a pillar of fire
the sea yawns
birth canal
labyrinth
blood-painted door

we enter joyful
that the future is just ahead

we enter afraid
of what pursues us

we enter
present with not knowing

we have escaped slavery
just barely
someone bought our freedom
we're not sure who
ancestors
children
prophets
the all-weaver
the angel of death

to either side
the water is mirrors
is windows
is a view of the deep

just ahead
is darkness
is a light shining
is the sound of singing
and the pounding of feet

(Rabbi Jill Hammer)

Hashkiveinu / Shelter of Peace

הַשְׁכִּיבֵנוּ יהוה אֱלֹהֵינוּ לְשָׁלוֹם, Hashkiveinu יהוה, Eloheinu, l'shalom,
וְהַעֲמִידֵנוּ, מַלְכֵּנוּ, v'ha·amideinu, Malkeinu,
לְחַיִּים טוֹבִים וּלְשָׁלוֹם, l'chayim tovim ul'shalom,
וּפְרֹשׂ עָלֵינוּ סֻכַּת שְׁלוֹמֶךָ, ufros aleinu sukat sh'lomecha,
וְתַקְּנֵנוּ בְּעֵצָה טוֹבָה מִלְּפָנֶיךָ, v'tak'neinu b'eitzah tovah mil'fanecha,
וְהוֹשִׁיעֵנוּ לְמַעַן שְׁמֶךָ. v'hoshi·einu l'ma·an sh'mecha.
וְהָגֵן בַּעֲדֵנוּ, וְהָסֵר מֵעָלֵינוּ V'hagein ba·adeinu, v'haseir mei·aleinu
אוֹיֵב, דֶּבֶר, וְחֶרֶב, וְרָעָב, וְיָגוֹן, oyeiv, dever, v'cherev, v'ra·av v'yagon,
וְהָסֵר שָׂטָן מִלְּפָנֵינוּ וּמֵאַחֲרֵינוּ, v'haseir satan mil'faneinu umei·achareinu,
וּבְצֵל כְּנָפֶיךָ תַּסְתִּירֵנוּ. uvtzeil k'nafecha tastireinu.
כִּי אֵל שׁוֹמְרֵנוּ וּמַצִּילֵנוּ אָתָּה, Ki El shom'reinu umatzileinu atah,
כִּי אֵל מֶלֶךְ חַנּוּן וְרַחוּם אָתָּה. ki El Melech chanun v'rachum atah.
וּשְׁמֹר צֵאתֵנוּ וּבוֹאֵנוּ, Ushmor tzeiteinu uvo·einu,
לְחַיִּים וּלְשָׁלוֹם, l'chayim ulshalom,
מֵעַתָּה וְעַד עוֹלָם. mei·atah v'ad olam.
בָּרוּךְ אַתָּה, יהוה, Baruch atah, יהוה,
שׁוֹמֵר עַמּוֹ יִשְׂרָאֵל לָעַד. shomeir amo Yisra·el la·ad.

Help us to lie down in peace, יהוה our God,
and to arise again to life.
Spread over the world Your sheltering peace.
Direct us with Your guidance, and save us.
Protect and keep us from enmity, illness, violence, want, and sorrow.
Remove envy and recrimination from us;
help us to sidestep our internal adversary.
Shelter us in the shadow of Your wings,
for You are a protecting, redeeming God.
You are God, our source of grace and mercy.
Guard our going out and our coming in,
for life and for peace, now and forever.
Spread Your sheltering peace over us.
Blessed are You, יהוה,
who spreads a shelter of peace over all of Your people.

Places of Holiness, Places of Peace

After the night of exile in Mitzrayim,
the awakening to divine presence in the Mishkan.
After the darkness of Yerushalayim's siege,
the dawn of Yavneh's flowering.

Guide us from darkness to dawn,
from insecurity to serenity in an uncertain world.

God — HaMakom — is the place of holiness;
God is everywhere,
so everywhere can be made holy.
Shalom is the peace of wholeness;
to recognize God everywhere is
to sense the holiness hidden in the world's fragments,
to feel commanded to join the fragments back together into a whole,
into peace.

Teach us to frame the world in Your Mishkan,
that we might encounter divine presence everywhere.
Cover our sleep within Your sukkah of peace,
that we might awake to wholeness every morning.

Spread over all of us the shelter of Your peace
and an awareness of Your presence.

(Mark Nazimova)

HaMakom - One of the names of God, meaning The Place
Mitzrayim - Egypt
Sukkah - Shelter, booth
Yerushalayim - Jerusalem
Yavneh - The town established by the early Rabbis as a safe haven when Jerusalem was under siege, so that Rabbinic Judaism could continue developing as the Second Temple (along with Temple-centered Judaism) was about to be destroyed by the Romans.

Baruch יהוה L'olam / Blessed is the One Forever

בָּרוּךְ יהוה לְעוֹלָם, אָמֵן וְאָמֵן.　Baruch יהוה l'olam, amen v'amen.

בָּרוּךְ יהוה מִצִּיּוֹן　Baruch יהוה miTziyon,

שֹׁכֵן יְרוּשָׁלָיִם הַלְלוּ־יָהּ.　shochein Y'rushalayim, Hal'lu·Yah.

בָּרוּךְ יהוה אֱלֹהִים אֱלֹהֵי יִשְׂרָאֵל,　Baruch יהוה Elohim Elohei Yisra·el,

עֹשֵׂה נִפְלָאוֹת לְבַדּוֹ,　oseih nifla·ot levado,

וּבָרוּךְ שֵׁם כְּבוֹדוֹ לְעוֹלָם, וְיִמָּלֵא　uvaruch sheim k'vodo l'olam, v'yimalei

כְבוֹדוֹ אֶת כָּל הָאָרֶץ, אָמֵן וְאָמֵן.　ch'vodo et kol ha·aretz, amen v'amen.

יְהִי כְבוֹד יהוה לְעוֹלָם,　Y'hi kh'vod יהוה l'olam,

יִשְׂמַח יהוה בְּמַעֲשָׂיו.　yismach יהוה b'ma·asav.

יְהִי שֵׁם יהוה מְבֹרָךְ,　Y'hi sheim יהוה m'vorach,

מֵעַתָּה וְעַד עוֹלָם.　mei·ata v'ad olam.

כִּי לֹא יִטּשׁ יְיָ אֶת עַמּוֹ　Ki lo yitosh יהוה et amo

בַּעֲבוּר שְׁמוֹ הַגָּדוֹל,　ba·avur sh'mo hagadol,

כִּי הוֹאִיל יהוה　ki ho·il יהוה

לַעֲשׂוֹת אֶתְכֶם לוֹ לְעָם.　la·asot et·chem lo l'am.

וַיַּרְא כָּל הָעָם וַיִּפְּלוּ עַל פְּנֵיהֶם,　Vayar kol ha·am vayip'lu al p'neiheim,

וַיֹּאמְרוּ, יהוה הוּא הָאֱלֹהִים,　vayom'ru, יהוה Hu haElohim,

יהוה הוּא הָאֱלֹהִים.　יהוה Hu haElohim.

Blessed is the One forever, Amen and Amen.
Blessed is the One dwelling in Zion and Jerusalem, halleluyah.
Blessed is the One, the God of Israel, who alone does miracles.
Blessed is the Name of the One forever;
　may God's glory fill the earth, amen v'amen.
May God's glory extend forever; may God rejoice in God's creation.
May the name of the One be blessed, from now until forever.
God will not abandon God's people; we were made to be in relationship with God.
When we see God's greatness, we fall on our faces, declaring: God is God!

וְהָיָה יהוה לְמֶלֶךְ עַל כָּל הָאָרֶץ,   V'hayah יהוה lemelech al kol ha·aretz,
בַּיּוֹם הַהוּא   bayom hahu
יִהְיֶה יהוה אֶחָד וּשְׁמוֹ אֶחָד.   yihyeh יהוה echad ushmo echad.
יְהִי חַסְדְּךָ יהוה עָלֵינוּ,   Y'hi chasd'cha יהוה aleinu,
כַּאֲשֶׁר יִחַלְנוּ לָךְ.   ka·asher yichalnu lach.
הוֹשִׁיעֵנוּ יהוה, אֱלֹהֵינוּ,   Hoshi·einu יהוה, Eloheinu,
וְקַבְּצֵנוּ מִן הַגּוֹיִם,   v'kab'tzeinu min hagoyim,
לְהוֹדוֹת לְשֵׁם קָדְשֶׁךָ,   l'hodot l'sheim kodshecha,
לְהִשְׁתַּבֵּחַ בִּתְהִלָּתֶךָ.   l'histabei·ach bit·hilatecha.
כָּל גּוֹיִם אֲשֶׁר עָשִׂיתָ   Kol goyim asher asita
יָבוֹאוּ וְיִשְׁתַּחֲווּ לְפָנֶיךָ, אֲדֹנָי,   yavo·u v'yishtachavu l'fanecha, Adonai,
וִיכַבְּדוּ לִשְׁמֶךָ.   v'yichabdu l'shmecha.
כִּי גָדוֹל אַתָּה וְעֹשֵׂה נִפְלָאוֹת,   Ki gadol atah v'oseh nifla·ot,
אַתָּה אֱלֹהִים לְבַדֶּךָ.   atah Elohim levadecha
וַאֲנַחְנוּ עַמְּךָ וְצֹאן מַרְעִיתֶךָ,   va·anachnu am'cha v'tzon maritecha,
נוֹדֶה לְךָ לְעוֹלָם,   nodeh l'cha l'olam,
לְדוֹר וָדוֹר נְסַפֵּר תְּהִלָּתֶךָ.   ledor vador n'sapeir t'hilatecha.

God is sovereign over all the earth.
On that day, God will be One and God's name will be One.
May God's mercy be upon us as we make God's presence real for ourselves.
Save us, יהוה our God; gather us in, that we might praise Your name.
May all the peoples whom You have created
bend the knee before You and praise Your name.
For You are great; You do wonders, You alone.
And we are Your people, the flock that You tend; we thank You always,
and sing Your praises from generation to generation.

בָּרוּךְ יהוה בַּיּוֹם,   Baruch יהוה bayom,
בָּרוּךְ יהוה בַּלָּיְלָה,   baruch יהוה balailah,
בָּרוּךְ יהוה בְּשָׁכְבֵנוּ,   baruch יהוה b'shochveinu,
בָּרוּךְ יהוה בְּקוּמֵנוּ.   baruch יהוה b'kumeinu.
כִּי בְיָדְךָ נַפְשׁוֹת הַחַיִּים וְהַמֵּתִים,   Ki v'yad'cha nafshot hachayim v'hameitim,
אֲשֶׁר בְּיָדוֹ נֶפֶשׁ כָּל חָי   asher b'yado nefesh kol chai
וְרוּחַ כָּל בְּשַׂר אִישׁ.   v'ruach kol b'sar ish.
בְּיָדְךָ אַפְקִיד רוּחִי, פָּדִיתָה אוֹתִי,   B'yad'cha afkid ruchi, paditah oti,
יהוה, אֵל אֱמֶת.   יהוה, El emet.
אֱלֹהֵינוּ שֶׁבַּשָּׁמַיִם, יַחֵד שְׁמְךָ,   Eloheinu shebashamayim, yacheid shimcha,
וְקַיֵּם מַלְכוּתְךָ תָּמִיד,   v'kayeim malchut'cha tamid,
וּמְלוֹךְ עָלֵינוּ לְעוֹלָם וָעֶד.   umloch aleinu l'olam va·ed.

May the One be blessed by day and by night,
when we lie down and when we rise up.
For in Your hands are our lives and our deaths,
the breath of all life and the spirit of all flesh.
Into Your hands I place my spirit, O God of truth.
God Who is in the heavens: may Your name be unified,
may Your sovereignty endure always, may You rule over us always.

יְרְאוּ עֵינֵינוּ, וְיִשְׂמַח לִבֵּנוּ,   Yiru einenu, v'yismach libeinu,
וְתָגֵל נַפְשֵׁנוּ בִּישׁוּעָתְךָ בֶּאֱמֶת,   v'tageil nafsheinu bishuat'cha be·emet,
בֶּאֱמֹר לְצִיּוֹן, מָלַךְ אֱלֹהָיִךְ.   be·emor leTziyon, malach Elohayich.
יהוה מֶלֶךְ, יהוה מָלָךְ,   יהוה melech, יהוה malach,
יהוה יִמְלֹךְ לְעוֹלָם וָעֶד.   יהוה yimloch l'olam va·ed.
כִּי הַמַּלְכוּת שֶׁלְּךָ הִיא,   Ki hamalchut shel'cha hi,
וּלְעוֹלְמֵי עַד תִּמְלֹךְ בְּכָבוֹד,   ulol'mei ad timloch b'chavod,
כִּי אֵין לָנוּ מֶלֶךְ אֶלָּא אָתָּה.   ki ein lanu melech ela atah.
בָּרוּךְ אַתָּה יהוה, הַמֶּלֶךְ בִּכְבוֹדוֹ,   Baruch atah יהוה, hamelech bichvodo,
תָּמִיד יִמְלֹךְ עָלֵינוּ לְעוֹלָם וָעֶד,   tamid yimloch aleinu l'olam va·ed,
וְעַל כָּל מַעֲשָׂיו.   v'al kol maasav.

May our eyes see you, and may our hearts rejoice,
and may our souls know your redemption in truth,
flowing from Zion, O our sovereign and our God.
God reigned then, God reigns now,
God will reign forever and ever.
For sovereignty is Yours,
and You will reign always in glory;
we have no God but You.
Blessed are You, יהוה, who reigns in glory;
You will reign over us always,
and over all of Your creations.

The Kaddish: A Door

In all of its forms, the Kaddish is a doorway
between one part of the service and the next.

As we move through this door, notice:
what is happening in your heart and mind?

Whatever is arising in you,
bring that into your prayer.

Chatzi Kaddish / Half Kaddish

יִתְגַּדַּל וְיִתְקַדַּשׁ שְׁמֵהּ רַבָּא,
Yitgadal v'yitkadash sh'meih raba,

בְּעָלְמָא דִּי בְרָא כִרְעוּתֵהּ,
b'al'ma di v'ra chiruteih,

וְיַמְלִיךְ מַלְכוּתֵהּ,
v'yamlich malchuteih,

בְּחַיֵּיכוֹן וּבְיוֹמֵיכוֹן
b'chayeichon uvyomeichon,

וּבְחַיֵּי דְכָל בֵּית יִשְׂרָאֵל,
uvchayei d'chol beit Yisra·el,

בַּעֲגָלָא וּבִזְמַן קָרִיב,
ba·agala uvizman kariv,

וְאִמְרוּ: **אָמֵן.**
v'imru: **Amen.**

יְהֵא שְׁמֵהּ רַבָּא מְבָרַךְ
Y'hei sh'meih raba m'varach

לְעָלַם וּלְעָלְמֵי עָלְמַיָּא.
l'alam ulal'mei al'maya.

יִתְבָּרַךְ וְיִשְׁתַּבַּח וְיִתְפָּאַר
Yitbarach v'yishtabach v'yitpa·ar

וְיִתְרוֹמַם וְיִתְנַשֵּׂא וְיִתְהַדָּר
v'yit·romam v'yitnasei v'yit·hadar

וְיִתְעַלֶּה וְיִתְהַלָּל שְׁמֵהּ דְּקֻדְשָׁא,
v'yitaleh v'yit·halal sh'meih d'kudsha

בְּרִיךְ הוּא,
b'rich hu

לְעֵלָּא
l'eila

During the Ten Days of Repentance:

וּלְעֵלָּא
uleila

מִן כָּל בִּרְכָתָא וְשִׁירָתָא,
min kol birchata v'shirata,

תֻּשְׁבְּחָתָא וְנֶחֱמָתָא,
tushb'chata v'nechemata,

דַּאֲמִירָן בְּעָלְמָא, וְאִמְרוּ: אָמֵן.
da·amiran b'al'ma; v'imru: Amen.

Magnified and sanctified! Magnified and sanctified!
May God's Great Name fill the world God created.
May God's splendor be seen in the world in your life,
in your days, in the life of all Israel.
Quickly and soon!
And let us say: Amen.
Forever may the Great Name be blessed!
Blessed and praised! Splendid and supreme!
May the holy Name, Bless God, be praised,
(During the Ten Days of Repentance: far,)
far beyond all the blessings and songs,
comforts and consolations,
that can be offered in this world.
And let us say: Amen.

Amidah

In this service there are two versions of the weekday Amidah, the standing prayer that is at the heart of every Jewish service. First there is a contemplative version, in which we offer a *kavanah* or meditative focus for each of the Amidah's themes. Then there is the full-text version, which features the complete Hebrew text of the traditional prayer. Use whichever one best allows you to speak from your heart the words you most need to say to the One at this time.

The Contemplative Amidah follows here.
The Full-text Amidah appears on p. 95.

Meditation Before the Amidah

What do you most need to say to God tonight?

What do you need to pour forth from your heart?

What healing do you yearn for?

Contemplative Amidah

These are the themes of the Weekday Amidah.
Meditate on each of them in your own time.
If you wish to close each reflection with the closing words in Hebrew
that "seal" each blessing, they are here for your use.

Avot V'imahot / Ancestors
I reflect on my ancestors. Who did I come from? How did they shape me?
Baruch atah, יהוה, magein Avraham v'ezrat Sarah.
בָּרוּךְ אַתָּה, יהוה, מָגֵן אַבְרָהָם וְעֶזְרַת שָׂרָה.

Gevurot / Power
What is the source of power in my life?
Where do I find strength? What enlivens me?
Baruch atah, יהוה, m'chayeih hameitim.
בָּרוּךְ אַתָּה, יהוה, מְחַיֵּה הַמֵּתִים.

Kedushah / Holiness
I open myself to holiness.
I seek to live wholly and in a way that is holy.
Baruch atah, יהוה, ha·El hakadosh.
בָּרוּךְ אַתָּה, יהוה, הָאֵל הַקָּדוֹשׁ.

Binah / Understanding
I seek wisdom and understanding in my life.
Baruch atah, יהוה, chonein hada·at.
בָּרוּךְ אַתָּה, יהוה, חוֹנֵן הַדָּעַת.

T'shuvah / Return
I want to orient myself in the right direction,
to re/turn to my deepest self and my highest aspirations.
Baruch atah, יהוה, harotzeh bit·shuvah.
בָּרוּךְ אַתָּה, יהוה, הָרוֹצֶה בִּתְשׁוּבָה.

S'licha / Forgiveness
I aspire to cultivate forgiveness,
and I ask all those whom I have hurt to forgive me.
Baruch atah, יהוה, chanun hamarbeh lislo·ach.
בָּרוּךְ אַתָּה, יהוה, חַנּוּן הַמַּרְבֶּה לִסְלֹחַ.

Ge·ulah / Redemption

I ask the source of transformation to lift me out of my narrow places.
Baruch atah, יהוה, go·eil Yisra·el.

בָּרוּךְ אַתָּה, יהוה, גּוֹאֵל יִשְׂרָאֵל.

Refu·ah / Healing

Heal my wounded places. Help me be a source of healing for others.
Baruch atah, יהוה, rofei cholei amo Yisra·el.

בָּרוּךְ אַתָּה, יהוה, רוֹפֵא חוֹלֵי עַמּוֹ יִשְׂרָאֵל.

Birkat Hashanim / Cycles

May abundant blessing pour into creation in this turning of the wheel
and in all of the cycles of our lives.
Baruch atah, יהוה, m'varech hashanim.

בָּרוּךְ אַתָּה, יהוה, מְבָרֵךְ הַשָּׁנִים.

Kibutz Galuyot / Ingathering

May we be gathered in from our spiritual exile.
May this be true for us as individuals and for us as a people.
Baruch atah, יהוה, m'kabeitz nidchei amo Yisra·el.

בָּרוּךְ אַתָּה, יהוה, מְקַבֵּץ נִדְחֵי עַמּוֹ יִשְׂרָאֵל.

Din / Justice

May justice flow like waters
and righteousness like a mighty stream.
May we all be blessed with good judgment, discernment, and good boundaries.
Baruch atah, יהוה, melech oheiv tz'dakah umishpat.

בָּרוּךְ אַתָּה, יהוה, מֶלֶךְ אוֹהֵב צְדָקָה וּמִשְׁפָּט.

Birkat Haminim / Divisions

May unhelpful divisions be bridged and healed.
May wickedness come to its end. May hope and righteousness reign.
Baruch atah, יהוה, shoveir oyvim umachni·a zeidim.

בָּרוּךְ אַתָּה, יהוה, שֹׁבֵר אֹיְבִים וּמַכְנִיעַ זֵדִים.

Tzadikim / Righteous Ones

May all of my righteous and holy teachers be blessed.
May I recognize that the whole world can be my teacher.
Baruch atah, יהוה, mishan umivtach latzadikim.

בָּרוּךְ אַתָּה, יהוה, מִשְׁעָן וּמִבְטָח לַצַּדִּיקִים.

Boneih Yerushalayim / Jerusalem

May Jerusalem, our holy city of old, be blessed with wholeness and peace.
May her inhabitants relate to one another with righteousness and love.
May all places where humanity dwells be blessed.
Baruch atah, יהוה, boneih Yerushalayim.

בָּרוּךְ אַתָּה, יהוה, בּוֹנֶה יְרוּשָׁלָיִם.

Y'shu·a / A World Transformed

May redemption flower forth and transform our world
into a world where suffering, hatred, and loss are no more.
Baruch atah, יהוה, matzmi·ach keren y'shu·ah.

בָּרוּךְ אַתָּה, יהוה, מַצְמִיחַ קֶרֶן יְשׁוּעָה.

Sh'ma Koleinu / Hear Our Voices

May our prayers be heard on high and deep within.
May the deepest murmurings of our hearts be heard and honored.
Baruch atah, יהוה, shomei·a t'filah.

בָּרוּךְ אַתָּה, יהוה, שׁוֹמֵעַ תְּפִלָּה.

Avoda / Service

May my life be an expression of my desire to serve something greater than myself.
May my service help to uplift Shechinah, Divine presence, everywhere.
Baruch atah, יהוה, hamachazir shechinato leTziyon.

בָּרוּךְ אַתָּה, יהוה, הַמַּחֲזִיר שְׁכִינָתוֹ לְצִיּוֹן.

Hoda·ah / Gratitude

Help me to cultivate gratitude for the blessings of every day.
Baruch atah, יהוה, hatov shimcha ulcha na·eh l'hodot.

בָּרוּךְ אַתָּה, יהוה, הַטּוֹב שִׁמְךָ וּלְךָ נָאֶה לְהוֹדוֹת.

Shalom / Peace

Help me to feel and to embody peace and wholeness.
Baruch atah, יהוה, hamvareich et amo Yisra·el bashalom.

בָּרוּךְ אַתָּה, יהוה, הַמְבָרֵךְ אֶת עַמּוֹ יִשְׂרָאֵל בַּשָּׁלוֹם.

עֹשֶׂה שָׁלוֹם בִּמְרוֹמָיו   Oseh shalom bimromav,
הוּא יַעֲשֶׂה שָׁלוֹם עָלֵינוּ   hu ya·aseh shalom aleinu
וְעַל כָּל יִשְׂרָאֵל,   v'al kol Yisra·el,
וְעַל כָּל יוֹשְׁבֵי תֵבֵל,   v'al kol yoshvei teiveil,
וְאִמְרוּ: אָמֵן.   v'imru: Amen.

May the One who makes peace in the heavens
make peace for us, for all Israel,
and for all who dwell on earth.
And let us say: Amen.

Full-Text Amidah

אֲדֹנָי, שְׂפָתַי תִּפְתָּח,   Adonai, s'fatai tiftach,
וּפִי יַגִּיד תְּהִלָּתֶךָ.   ufi yagid t'hilatecha.

Eternal God, open my lips
that my mouth may declare Your praise.

Avot V'imahot / Ancestors

בָּרוּךְ אַתָּה, יהוה,   Baruch atah, יהוה,
אֱלֹהֵינוּ וֵאלֹהֵי אֲבוֹתֵינוּ   Eloheinu veilohei avoteinu
וְאִמּוֹתֵינוּ,   v'imoteinu,
אֱלֹהֵי אַבְרָהָם, אֱלֹהֵי יִצְחָק,   Elohei Avraham, Elohei Yitzchak,
וֵאלֹהֵי יַעֲקֹב;   veilohei Ya·akov;

some omit

אֱלֹהֵי שָׂרָה, אֱלֹהֵי רִבְקָה,   Elohei Sarah, Elohei Rivkah,
אֱלֹהֵי רָחֵל, וֵאלֹהֵי לֵאָה,   Elohei Racheil, veilohei Lei·ah,

הָאֵל הַגָּדוֹל הַגִּבּוֹר וְהַנּוֹרָא,   Ha·el hagadol hagibor v'hanora,
אֵל עֶלְיוֹן, גּוֹמֵל חֲסָדִים טוֹ   El elyon, gomeil chasadim tovim,
בִים, וְקֹנֵה הַכֹּל, וְזוֹכֵר חַסְדֵי אָבוֹת   v'konei hakol v'zocheir chasdei avot
וְאִמָּהוֹת,   v'imahot,
וּמֵבִיא גוֹאֵל לִבְנֵי בְנֵיהֶם,   umeivi go·eil livnei v'neihem,
לְמַעַן שְׁמוֹ בְּאַהֲבָה.   lema·an sh'mo b'ahavah.

Blessed are You, יהוה, our God and God of our ancestors,
God of Abraham, God of Isaac, God of Jacob;
God of Sarah, God of Rebecca, God of Rachel, and God of Leah;
the great, mighty, and awesome God,
God on high, who does deeds of lovingkindness,
who is the Source of all,
and who remembers the steadfast love of our ancestors,
who lovingly brings redemption to their children's children for Your name's sake.

During the Ten Days of Repentance
(between Rosh Hashanah and Yom Kippur)

זָכְרֵנוּ לְחַיִּים, Zochreinu l'chayim,

מֶלֶךְ חָפֵץ בַּחַיִּים, melech chafeitz bachayim,

וְכָתְבֵנוּ בְּסֵפֶר הַחַיִּים, v'chotveinu b'sefer hachayim,

לְמַעַנְךָ אֱלֹהִים חַיִּים. lema·ancha Elohim chayim.

Remember us for life, Sovereign who chooses life,
and inscribe us in the book of life for Your sake, God of life.

מֶלֶךְ עוֹזֵר וּמוֹשִׁיעַ וּמָגֵן. Melech ozeir umoshi·a umagen.

בָּרוּךְ אַתָּה, יהוה, Baruch atah, יהוה,

מָגֵן אַבְרָהָם וְעֶזְרַת שָׂרָה. magein Avraham v'ezrat Sarah.

Ruler, Helper, Redeemer, and Protector,
blessed are You, Abraham's shield and Sarah's strength.

Gevurot / Strength

אַתָּה גִּבּוֹר לְעוֹלָם יהוה, Atah gibor l'olam יהוה,

מְחַיֵּה מֵתִים אַתָּה, רַב לְהוֹשִׁיעַ. m'chayei meitim atah rav l'hoshi·a.

בקיץ: מוֹרִיד הַטָּל. Summer: Morid hatal.

בחורף: מַשִּׁיב הָרוּחַ וּמוֹרִיד הַגֶּשֶׁם. Winter: Mashiv haruach umorid hageshem.

You are our eternal strength, יהוה.
Your saving power gives life that transcends death.
Summer: You bring the dew of the field.
Winter: You cause the winds to blow and the rains to fall.

מְכַלְכֵּל חַיִּים בְּחֶסֶד,   Mechalkeil chayim b'chesed,
מְחַיֵּה מֵתִים בְּרַחֲמִים רַבִּים,   m'chayei meitim b'rachamim rabim,
סוֹמֵךְ נוֹפְלִים, וְרוֹפֵא חוֹלִים,   someich nof'lim, v'rofei cholim,
וּמַתִּיר אֲסוּרִים,   umatir asurim,
וּמְקַיֵּם אֱמוּנָתוֹ לִישֵׁנֵי עָפָר.   umkayeim emunato lisheinei afar.
מִי כָמוֹךָ בַּעַל גְּבוּרוֹת,   Mi chamocha baal g'vurot,
וּמִי דּוֹמֶה לָּךְ,   Umi domeh lach?
מֶלֶךְ מֵמִית וּמְחַיֶּה   Melech meimit umchayei,
וּמַצְמִיחַ יְשׁוּעָה.   umatzmi·ach y'shu·ah.

וְנֶאֱמָן אַתָּה לְהַחֲיוֹת מֵתִים.   V'ne·eman atah l'hachayot meitim.
בָּרוּךְ אַתָּה, יהוה,   Baruch atah, יהוה,
מְחַיֵּה הַמֵּתִים.   m'chayei hameitim.

You sustain the living with kindness;
in Your great mercy You bestow eternal life.
You support the fallen, heal the sick, and free the captive.
You keep Your faith with us beyond life and death.
There is none like You, our source of strength,
the ruler of life and death, the source of our redemption.

Who is like You, Source of Mercy,
Who mercifully remembers Your creatures for life?
Our faith is with You, the God Who brings eternal life.
Blessed are You, יהוה, Who gives life which transcends death.

During the Ten Days of Repentance
(between Rosh Hashanah and Yom Kippur)

מִי כָמוֹךָ אַב הָרַחֲמִם,   Mi chamocha, av harachamim,
זוֹכֵר יְצוּרָיו לְחַיִּים בְּרַחֲמִים.   zocheir y'tzurav l'chayim b'rachamim.

Who is like You, Merciful Parent?
You remember us for life and for compassion!

Kidushat HaShem / Sanctification of God's Name

אַתָּה קָדוֹשׁ וְשִׁמְךָ קָדוֹשׁ,　Atah kadosh v'shimcha kadosh
וּקְדוֹשִׁים בְּכָל יוֹם יְהַלְלוּךָ סֶּלָה.　ukdoshim b'chol yom y'hal'lucha selah.
כִּי אֵל מֶלֶךְ גָּדוֹל וְקָדוֹשׁ אָתָּה.　Ki El melech gadol v'kadosh atah.
*בָּרוּךְ אַתָּה, יהוה, הָאֵל הַקָּדוֹשׁ.　Baruch atah, יהוה, haEl haKadosh.

---

*During the Ten Days of Repentance:

בָּרוּךְ אַתָּה, יהוה, הַמֶּלֶךְ הַקָּדוֹשׁ.　Baruch atah, יהוה, ha·Melech hakadosh.

You are holy, and Your name is holy,
and holy ones praise You always.
*Blessed are You, יהוה, the holy God.

---

*During the Ten Days of Repentance: Blessed are You, יהוה, the holy King.

Bakashot / Weekday requests

אַתָּה חוֹנֵן לְאָדָם דַּעַת,　Atah chonein l'adam da·at,
וּמְלַמֵּד לֶאֱנוֹשׁ בִּינָה.　umlameid le·enosh binah.
חָנֵּנוּ מֵאִתְּךָ　Choneinu mei·it'cha
דֵּעָה בִּינָה וְהַשְׂכֵּל.　dei·ah binah v'haskeil.
בָּרוּךְ אַתָּה, יהוה, חוֹנֵן הַדָּעַת.　Baruch atah, יהוה, chonein hada·at.

You give humanity wisdom and teach us understanding.
Grace us with wisdom, insight, and knowledge.
Blessed are You, יהוה, who graces us with wisdom.

הֲשִׁיבֵנוּ, אָבִינוּ, לְתוֹרָתֶךָ,　Hashiveinu, avinu, l'toratecha,
וְקָרְבֵנוּ, מַלְכֵּנוּ, לַעֲבוֹדָתֶךָ,　v'kar'veinu, malkeinu, la·avodatecha,
וְהַחֲזִירֵנוּ　v'hachazireinu
בִּתְשׁוּבָה שְׁלֵמָה לְפָנֶיךָ.　bit·shuvah sh'leimah l'fanecha.
בָּרוּךְ אַתָּה, יהוה,　Baruch atah, יהוה,
הָרוֹצֶה בִּתְשׁוּבָה.　harotzeh bit·shuvah.

Return us, our Parent, to Your Torah;
draw us near, our Sovereign, to Your service;
help us to return in complete t'shuvah before You.
Blessed are You, יהוה, who wishes for our t'shuvah.

סְלַח לָנוּ, אָבִינוּ, כִּי חָטָאנוּ; S'lach lanu, avinu, ki chatanu;

מְחַל לָנוּ, מַלְכֵּנוּ, כִּי פָשָׁעְנוּ, m'chal lanu, malkeinu, ki fashanu;

כִּי מוֹחֵל וְסוֹלֵחַ אָתָּה. ki mocheil v'solei·ach atah.

בָּרוּךְ אַתָּה יהוה, Baruch atah, יהוה,

חַנּוּן הַמַּרְבֶּה לִסְלֹחַ. chanun hamarbeh lislo·ach.

Forgive us, our Parent, for we have sinned;
pardon us, our Sovereign, for we have erred;
for You are the one who forgives and pardons.
Blessed are You, יהוה, who graciously forgives.

רְאֵה נָא בְעָנְיֵנוּ, וְרִיבָה רִיבֵנוּ, R'eih na v'onyeinu, v'rivah riveinu,

וּגְאָלֵנוּ מְהֵרָה לְמַעַן שְׁמֶךָ, ugaleinu m'heirah l'ma·an sh'mecha,

כִּי גוֹאֵל חָזָק אָתָּה. ki goeil chazak atah.

בָּרוּךְ אַתָּה, יהוה, גּוֹאֵל יִשְׂרָאֵל. Baruch atah, יהוה, go·eil Yisra·el.

Take note of our affliction and our struggles.
Redeem us swiftly for Your name's sake.
Blessed are You, יהוה, Redeemer of Israel.

רְפָאֵנוּ, יהוה, וְנֵרָפֵא; R'fa·einu, יהוה, v'neirafei;

הוֹשִׁיעֵנוּ וְנִוָּשֵׁעָה, hoshi·einu v'nivashei·ah,

כִּי תְהִלָּתֵנוּ אָתָּה, ki t'hilateinu atah,

וְהַעֲלֵה רְפוּאָה שְׁלֵמָה v'haaleih r'fuah sh'leimah

לְכָל מַכּוֹתֵינוּ. l'chol makoteinu.

כִּי אֵל מֶלֶךְ רוֹפֵא נֶאֱמָן Ki El Melech rofei ne·eman

וְרַחֲמָן אָתָּה. v'rachaman atah.

בָּרוּךְ אַתָּה, יהוה, Baruch atah, יהוה,

רוֹפֵא חוֹלֵי עַמּוֹ יִשְׂרָאֵל. rofei cholei amo Yisra·el.

Heal us, יהוה, and we will be healed;
save us, and let us be saved;
for You are the healer,
and from You complete healing rises for every wound.
Blessed are You, יהוה, healer of the sick among Your people.

בָּרֵךְ עָלֵינוּ, יהוה אֱלֹהֵינוּ,   Bareich aleinu, יהוה Eloheinu,
אֶת הַשָּׁנָה הַזֹּאת   et hashanah hazot
וְאֶת כָּל מִינֵי תְבוּאָתָהּ לְטוֹבָה,   v'et kol minei t'vuatah l'tovah

in winter

וְתֵן טַל וּמָטָר לִבְרָכָה   v'tein tal umatar livrachah

in summer

וְתֵן בְּרָכָה   v'tein b'rachah

עַל פְּנֵי הָאֲדָמָה, וְשַׂבְּעֵנוּ מִטּוּבָהּ,   al p'nei ha·adamah, v'sab'einu mituvah,
וּבָרֵךְ שְׁנָתֵנוּ   uvareich sh'nateinu
כַּשָּׁנִים הַטּוֹבוֹת.   kashanim hatovot.
בָּרוּךְ אַתָּה, יהוה, מְבָרֵךְ הַשָּׁנִים.   Baruch atah, יהוה, m'vareich hashanim.

Bless, יהוה, our God, the cycle of this year
and all the various good things which grow.
And
in winter: grant blessing
in summer: grant the blessing of the dew
on the face of the earth.
Satisfy us with Your goodness, and bless this year as all good years.
Blessed are You, יהוה, who blesses the cycle of the years.

תְּקַע בְּשׁוֹפָר גָּדוֹל לְחֵרוּתֵנוּ,   T'ka b'shofar gadol l'cheiruteinu,
וְשָׂא נֵס לְקַבֵּץ גָּלֻיּוֹתֵינוּ,   v'sa neis l'kabeitz galuyoteinu,
וְקַבְּצֵנוּ יַחַד מְהֵרָה   v'kab'tzeinu yachad m'heirah
מֵאַרְבַּע כַּנְפוֹת הָאָרֶץ.   mei·arba kanfot ha·aretz.
בָּרוּךְ אַתָּה, יהוה,   Baruch atah, יהוה,
מְקַבֵּץ נִדְחֵי עַמּוֹ יִשְׂרָאֵל.   m'kabeitz nidchei amo Yisra·el.

Sound the great shofar for our freedom,
raise a banner for the oppressed,
gather us in from the four corners of the earth.
Blessed are You, יהוה, who ingathers the exiles of Your people.

הָשִׁיבָה שׁוֹפְטֵינוּ כְּבָרִאשׁוֹנָה Hashivah shof'teinu k'varishonah
וְיוֹעֲצֵינוּ כְּבַתְּחִלָּה, v'yo·atzeinu k'vat'chilah,
וְהָסֵר מִמֶּנּוּ יָגוֹן וַאֲנָחָה, v'haseir mimenu yagon va'anachah,
וּמְלוֹךְ עָלֵינוּ מְהֵרָה אַתָּה, יהוה, umloch aleinu m'heirah atah, יהוה,
לְבַדְּךָ בְּחֶסֶד וּבְרַחֲמִים, levad'cha b'chesed uvrachamim,
וְצַדְּקֵנוּ בַּמִּשְׁפָּט. v'tzadkeinu bamishpat.
בָּרוּךְ אַתָּה, יהוה, Baruch atah, יהוה,
מֶלֶךְ אוֹהֵב צְדָקָה וּמִשְׁפָּט. melech oheiv tz'dakah umishpat.

Let our judges be righteous, as they were of old;
bring mercy and lovingkindness through them;
for You are our ultimate ruler,
You alone in Your mercy and compassion,
your justice and your statutes.
Blessed are You, יהוה, Ruler who loves justice.

וְלַמַּלְשִׁינוּת אַל תְּהִי תִקְוָה, V'lamalshinut al t'hi tikvah,
וְכָל הָרִשְׁעָה כְּרֶגַע תֹּאבֵד, v'chol harisha k'rega toveid,
וְכָל אֹיְבֶיךָ מְהֵרָה יִכָּרֵתוּ, v'chol oy'vecha m'heirah yikareitu,
וְהַזֵּדִים מְהֵרָה תְעַקֵּר וּתְשַׁבֵּר v'hazeidim m'heirah t'akeir ut·shabeir
וּתְמַגֵּר וְתַכְנִיעַ בִּמְהֵרָה בְיָמֵינוּ. utmageir v'tachni·a bimheirah v'yameinu.
בָּרוּךְ אַתָּה, יהוה, Baruch atah, יהוה,
שׁוֹבֵר אֹיְבִים וּמַכְנִיעַ זֵדִים. shoveir oy'vim umachni·a zeidim.

And may wickedness not be given hope,
and may the errant return to You, speedily and in our days.
Blessed are You, יהוה, who shatters wickedness.

עַל הַצַּדִּיקִים וְעַל הַחֲסִידִים Al hatzadikim v'al hachasidim
וְעַל זִקְנֵי עַמְּךָ בֵּית יִשְׂרָאֵל, v'al ziknei am'cha beit Yisra·el,
וְעַל פְּלֵיטַת סוֹפְרֵיהֶם, v'al p'leitat sof'reihem,
וְעַל גֵּרֵי הַצֶּדֶק וְעָלֵינוּ, v'al gerei hatzedek v'aleinu,
יֶהֱמוּ נָא רַחֲמֶיךָ, יהוה אֱלֹהֵינוּ, yehemu na rachamecha יהוה Eloheinu,
וְתֵן שָׂכָר טוֹב v'tein sachar tov
לְכָל הַבּוֹטְחִים בְּשִׁמְךָ בֶּאֱמֶת, l'chol habot'chim b'shimcha be·emet,
וְשִׂים חֶלְקֵנוּ עִמָּהֶם, v'sim chelkeinu imahem,
וּלְעוֹלָם לֹא נֵבוֹשׁ ulolam lo neivosh
כִּי בְךָ בָּטָחְנוּ. ki v'cha batachnu.
בָּרוּךְ אַתָּה, יהוה, Baruch atah, יהוה,
מִשְׁעָן וּמִבְטָח לַצַּדִּיקִים. mishan umivtach latzadikim.

And on the righteous ones and the pious ones and our elders,
and on our leaders, and on the strangers who dwell among us,
and on us, may you grant compassion, יהוה our God,
and give blessing and good reward to all who trust in Your name,
and number us among them forever,
and let us never waver from our faith in You.
Blessed are You, יהוה, the staff and stay of the righteous.

וְלִירוּשָׁלַיִם עִירְךָ בְּרַחֲמִים תָּשׁוּב, V'lirushalayim ir'cha b'rachamim tashuv,
וְתִשְׁכּוֹן בְּתוֹכָהּ כַּאֲשֶׁר דִּבַּרְתָּ, v'tishkon b'tochah ka·asher dibarta,
וּבְנֵה אוֹתָהּ בְּקָרוֹב בְּיָמֵינוּ uvneih otah b'karov b'yameinu
בִּנְיַן עוֹלָם, binyan olam,
וְכִסֵּא דָוִד מְהֵרָה לְתוֹכָהּ תָּכִין. v'chisei David m'heirah l'tochah tachin.
בָּרוּךְ אַתָּה, יהוה, Baruch atah, יהוה,
בּוֹנֵה יְרוּשָׁלָיִם. boneih Y'rushalayim.

And to Jerusalem Your city speedily return in compassion.
Help us to rebuild her speedily and in our days,
in a manner befitting the throne of David.
Give rest to Zion and help us to rebuild Jerusalem.
Blessed are You, יהוה, builder of Jerusalem.

אֶת צֶמַח דָּוִד עַבְדְּךָ Et tzemach David avd'cha
מְהֵרָה תַצְמִיחַ, m'heirah tatzmiach,
וְקַרְנוֹ תָּרוּם בִּישׁוּעָתֶךָ, v'karno tarum bishuatecha,
כִּי לִישׁוּעָתְךָ קִוִּינוּ כָּל הַיּוֹם. ki lishu·at'cha kivinu kol hayom.
בָּרוּךְ אַתָּה, יהוה, Baruch atah, יהוה,
מַצְמִיחַ קֶרֶן יְשׁוּעָה. matzmiach keren y'shu·ah.

May the sprout of David flower forth,
bringing with it Your redemption,
for we hope for Your redemption every day.
Blessed are You, יהוה, who brings forth redemption.

שְׁמַע קוֹלֵנוּ, יהוה אֱלֹהֵינוּ, Sh'ma koleinu, יהוה Eloheinu,
חוּס וְרַחֵם עָלֵינוּ, וְקַבֵּל בְּרַחֲמִים chus v'racheim aleinu, v'kabeil b'rachamim
וּבְרָצוֹן אֶת תְּפִלָּתֵנוּ, uvratzon et t'filateinu,
כִּי אֵל שׁוֹמֵעַ תְּפִלּוֹת ki El shomei·a t'filot
וְתַחֲנוּנִים אָתָּה, v'tachanunim atah,
וּמִלְּפָנֶיךָ, מַלְכֵּנוּ, umil'fanecha, malkeinu,
רֵיקָם אַל תְּשִׁיבֵנוּ. reikam al t'shiveinu.
כִּי אַתָּה שׁוֹמֵעַ Ki atah shomei·a
תְּפִלַּת עַמְּךָ יִשְׂרָאֵל בְּרַחֲמִים. t'filat am'cha Yisra·el b'rachamim.
בָּרוּךְ אַתָּה יהוה, שׁוֹמֵעַ תְּפִלָּה. Baruch atah, יהוה, shomei·a t'filah.

Hear our words, יהוה our God,
be compassionate and merciful upon us,
and let our prayers be received with mercy according to Your will,
for You are the one who hears our prayers and supplications
that arise before You.
You are the one
who hears the prayers of Your people Israel with compassion.
Blessed are You, יהוה, hearer of prayer.

רְצֵה, יהוה אֱלֹהֵינוּ, בְּעַמְּךָ יִשְׂרָאֵל, R'tzei, יהוה Eloheinu, b'am'cha Yisra·el,
וְהָשֵׁב אֶת הָעֲבוֹדָה לִדְבִיר בֵּיתֶךָ, v'hasheiv et ha·avodah lidvir beitecha,
וְאִשֵּׁי יִשְׂרָאֵל, וּתְפִלָּתָם v'ishei Yisra·el, utfilatam
מְהֵרָה בְּאַהֲבָה תְקַבֵּל בְּרָצוֹן, m'heirah b'ahavah t'kabeil b'ratzon,
וּתְהִי לְרָצוֹן תָּמִיד ut·hi l'ratzon tamid
עֲבוֹדַת יִשְׂרָאֵל עַמֶּךָ. avodat Yisra·el amecha.

Accept, יהוה our God, the prayers of Your people Israel;
find favor in us and accept our prayers in love.
May our prayers always ascend to You in love.

On Rosh Chodesh, and on the intermediate days of festivals:

אֱלֹהֵֽינוּ וֵאלֹהֵי אֲבוֹתֵֽינוּ   Eloheinu veilohei avoteinu

וְאִמּוֹתֵֽינוּ,   v'imoteinu,

יַעֲלֶה וְיָבֹא, וְיַגִּֽיעַ, וְיֵרָאֶה,   ya·aleh v'yavo, v'yagi·a, v'yeira·eh,

וְיֵרָצֶה, וְיִשָּׁמַע, וְיִפָּקֵד,   v'yeiratzeh, v'yishama, v'yipakeid,

וְיִזָּכֵר זִכְרוֹנֵֽנוּ וּפִקְדוֹנֵֽנוּ,   v'yizacheir zichroneinu ufikdoneinu,

וְזִכְרוֹן אֲבוֹתֵֽינוּ וְאִמּוֹתֵֽינוּ,   v'zichron avoteinu v'imoteinu,

וְזִכְרוֹן מָשִׁיחַ בֶּן דָּוִד עַבְדֶּֽךָ,   v'zichron mashi·ach ben David avdecha,

וְזִכְרוֹן יְרוּשָׁלַֽיִם עִיר קָדְשֶֽׁךָ,   vzichron Yerushalayim ir kodshecha,

וְזִכְרוֹן כָּל עַמְּךָ בֵּית יִשְׂרָאֵל לְפָנֶֽיךָ,   v'zichron kol am'cha beit Yisra·el l'fanecha,

לִפְלֵיטָה, לְטוֹבָה, לְחֵן וּלְחֶֽסֶד   lifleitah, l'tovah, l'chein ulchesed

וּלְרַחֲמִים, לְחַיִּים וּלְשָׁלוֹם, בְּיוֹם   ulrachamim, l'chayim ulshalom, b'yom

לְרֹאשׁ חֹֽדֶשׁ: רֹאשׁ הַחֹֽדֶשׁ הַזֶּה.   Rosh Chodesh: **Rosh haChodesh hazeh.**

לְפֶֽסַח: חַג הַמַּצּוֹת הַזֶּה.   Pesach: **Chag haMatzot hazeh.**

לְסֻכּוֹת: חַג הַסֻּכּוֹת הַזֶּה.   Sukkot: **Chag haSukkot hazeh.**

זָכְרֵֽנוּ, יהוה, אֱלֹהֵֽינוּ, בּוֹ לְטוֹבָה,   Zochreinu, יהוה Eloheinu, bo l'tova,

וּפָקְדֵֽנוּ בוֹ לִבְרָכָה,   ufokdeinu vo livrachah,

וְהוֹשִׁיעֵֽנוּ בוֹ לְחַיִּים,   v'hoshi·einu vo l'chayim,

וּבִדְבַר יְשׁוּעָה וְרַחֲמִים,   uvidvar yeshu·ah v'rachamim,

חוּס וְחָנֵּֽנוּ, וְרַחֵם עָלֵֽינוּ   chus v'choneinu, v'rachem aleinu

וְהוֹשִׁיעֵֽנוּ, כִּי אֵלֶֽיךָ עֵינֵֽינוּ,   v'hoshi·einu, ki eilecha eineinu,

כִּי אֵל מֶֽלֶךְ חַנּוּן וְרַחוּם אָֽתָּה.   ki El Melech chanun v'rachum atah.

On Rosh Chodesh, and on the intermediate days of festivals:

Our God and God of our ancestors:
allow memory to ascend,
to come, to reach us.
May our memory
and our ancestors' memory
and the memory of the dream
of a messianic time,
and the memory of the vision
of Jerusalem as a city of peace,
and the memories of all of Your people
of the House of Israel,
be before You

on this day of (Rosh Chodesh) (Pesach) (Sukkot).

On this day
may these memories,
these dreams of redemption,
inspire graciousness, lovingkindness,
and compassion in us,
for life and for peace.
Remember us, יהוה our God, for goodness.
Count us in for blessing.
Save us with life.
Shower us with salvation
and with compassion;
be merciful to us; enfold us
in the compassion we knew
before we were born.
For You are our merciful Parent and Sovereign.

וְתֶחֱזֶינָה עֵינֵינוּ   V'techezenah eineinu

בְּשׁוּבְךָ לְצִיּוֹן בְּרַחֲמִים.   b'shuv'cha leTziyon b'rachamim.

בָּרוּךְ אַתָּה, יהוה,   Baruch atah, יהוה,

הַמַּחֲזִיר שְׁכִינָתוֹ לְצִיּוֹן.   hamachazir shechinato leTziyon.

May our eyes see Your presence
return to Zion with compassion.
Blessed are You, יהוה, whose Presence returns to Zion

מוֹדִים אֲנַחְנוּ לָךְ, שָׁאַתָּה הוּא,   Modim anachnu lach, sha·atah hu,

יהוה אֱלֹהֵינוּ   יהוה Eloheinu

וֵאלֹהֵי אֲבוֹתֵינוּ וְאִמּוֹתֵינוּ   veilohei avoteinu v'imoteinu,

לְעוֹלָם וָעֶד, צוּרֵנוּ צוּר חַיֵּינוּ,   l'olam va·ed, tzureinu tzur chayeinu,

מָגֵן יִשְׁעֵנוּ, אַתָּה הוּא   magein yisheinu, atah hu

לְדוֹר וָדוֹר,   ledor vador,

נוֹדֶה לְךָ וּנְסַפֵּר תְּהִלָּתֶךָ,   nodeh l'cha unsaper t'hilatecha,

עַל חַיֵּינוּ הַמְּסוּרִים בְּיָדֶךָ,   al chayeinu ham'surim b'yadecha,

וְעַל נִשְׁמוֹתֵינוּ הַפְּקוּדוֹת לָךְ,   v'al nishmoteinu hap'kudot lach,

וְעַל נִסֶּיךָ שֶׁבְּכָל יוֹם עִמָּנוּ,   v'al nisecha sheb'chol yom imanu,

וְעַל נִפְלְאוֹתֶיךָ וְטוֹבוֹתֶיךָ   v'al nifl'otecha v'tovotecha

שֶׁבְּכָל עֵת, עֶרֶב וָבֹקֶר וְצָהֳרָיִם,   sheb'chol eit, erev vavoker v'tzohorayim,

הַטּוֹב, כִּי לֹא כָלוּ רַחֲמֶיךָ,   hatov, ki lo chalu rachamecha,

וְהַמְרַחֵם, כִּי לֹא תַמּוּ חֲסָדֶיךָ,   v'hamracheim, ki lo tamu chasadecha,

כִּי מֵעוֹלָם קִוִּינוּ לָךְ.   ki mei·olam kivinu lach.

We are grateful before You,
for You, יהוה our God and God of our ancestors,
are forever the rock of our lives, the shield of our salvation;
You are this for us in every generation.
For our lives, which are in Your hands,
and our souls, which are in Your keeping,
and for the wonders You do for us each day
and the miracles You perform for us at every moment,
evening and morning and afternoon:
Your mercies never end, Your compassion never fails, we put our hope in You.

On Chanukah and Purim

עַל הַנִּסִּים, וְעַל הַפֻּרְקָן,　Al hanisim, v'al hapurkan,
וְעַל הַגְּבוּרוֹת, וְעַל הַתְּשׁוּעוֹת,　v'al hag'vurot, v'al hat'shu·ot,
וְעַל הַנִּפְלָאוֹת,　v'al hanifla·ot,
שֶׁעָשִׂיתָ לַאֲבוֹתֵינוּ וּלְאִמּוֹתֵינוּ　she·asita la·avoteinu ulimoteinu
בַּיָּמִים הָהֵם בַּזְּמַן הַזֶּה.　bayamim haheim baz'man hazeh.

For the miracles, for the redemption,
for the mighty deeds, for the saving acts,
and for the wonders, which You wrought for our ancestors
in those days, at this time.

On Chanukah

בִּימֵי מַתִּתְיָהוּ כֹּהֵן גָּדוֹל　Bimei Mattityahu kohein gadol
חַשְׁמוֹנַאי וּבָנָיו כְּשֶׁעָמְדָה עֲלֵיהֶם　chashmonai uvanav k'she·amd'a aleihem
מַלְכוּת אַנְטִיוֹכוֹס הָרָשָׁע　malchut Antiyochos harasha
וּבִקֵּשׁ לַעֲקוֹר אֶת אֱמוּנָתֵינוּ　uvikeish la·akor et emunateinu
וְדָתֵנוּ וְהֵצֵרוּ לָנוּ וְכָבְשׁוּ אֶת　v'dateinu v'heitzeiru lanu v'chav'shu et
הֵיכָלֵנוּ טִמְּאוּ אֶת מִקְדָּשֵׁנוּ.　heichaleinu tim'u et mikdasheinu.
אָז קָמוּ נֶגְדָּם חֲסִידֶיךָ וְכֹהֲנֶיךָ,　Az kamu negdam chasidecha v'chohanecha,
וְאַתָּה, בְּרַחֲמֶיךָ הָרַבִּים,　v'atah, b'rachamecha harabim,
עָמַדְתָּ לָהֶם בְּעֵת צָרָתָם,　amadta lahem b'eit tzaratam,
רַבְתָּ אֶת רִיבָם, נָקַמְתָּ אֶת　ravta et rivam, nakamta et
נִקְמָתָם, וְהָיִיתָ בְּעֶזְרָתָם לְהִתְגַּבֵּר　nikmatam, v'hayita b'ezratam l'hitgabeir
עֲלֵיהֶם וּלְטַהֵר אֶת הַמִּקְדָּשׁ.　aleihem ultaheir et hamikdash.
מִתּוֹךְ גַּעֲגוּעִים לְהַשְׁרָאָתְךָ　Mitoch ga·agu·im l'hashra·at'cha
רָצוּ לְהַדְלִיק אֶת הַמְּנוֹרָה　ratzu l'hadlik et hamenorah
הַטְּהוֹרָה וְלֹא מָצְאוּ שֶׁמֶן　hat'horah v'lo matz'u shemen
עַד שֶׁהֶרְאֵיתָ לָהֶם שֶׁמֶן טָהוֹר　ad shehereita lahem shemen tahor
לְיוֹם אֶחָד. בְּבִטָּחוֹן הִדְלִיקוּ　l'yom echad. B'vitachon hidliku
אֶת הַמְּנוֹרָה וְאַתָּה עָשִׂיתָ לָהֶם　et hamenorah v'atah asita lahem
נֵס וָפֶלֶא, וְהַשֶּׁמֶן לֹא הִפְסִיק　neis vafeleh v'hashemen lo hifsik
עַד שֶׁעָשׂוּ מֵחָדָשׁ.　ad she·asu meichadash.
וְקָבְעוּ שְׁמוֹנַת יְמֵי חֲנֻכָּה אֵלוּ　V'kav'u sh'monat y'mei chanukah eilu
לְהַדְלִיק נֵרוֹת לְפִרְסוּם הַנֵּס　l'hadlik neirot l'firsum haneis
לְהוֹדוֹת בְּהַלֵּל לְשִׁמְךָ הַגָּדוֹל　l'hodot b'hallel l'shimcha hagadol
וְהַקָּדוֹשׁ עַל נִסֶּיךָ　v'hakadosh al nisecha
וְעַל נִפְלְאוֹתֶךָ וְעַל יְשׁוּעָתֶךָ.　v'al nifl'otecha v'al y'shu·atecha.

On Chanukah

In the days of Mattityahu, High priest, and his sons, when there arose against them the reign of wicked Antiochus, who sought to uproot our faith and law, oppressing us, they conquered our Temple and desecrated our sanctuary. Then there arose, against them, Your devout priests, and You, in Your great compassion, stood by them, in their troubles, waging their wars, avenging their pain, helping them to overcome Antiochus' forces and to purify the sanctuary. Amidst their longing for Your Presence among them, they sought to kindle the pure lamp and, not finding enough pure oil, You led them to find some, just enough for one day. In trust, they kindled the lamp, and You miraculously made the oil last until they could make some afresh. Then did they set these days of Chanukah to lighting candles, to chanting the Hallel, in gratitude to Your great reputation for Your miracles, Your wonders, and Your salvation.

(Adaptation and translation by Rabbi Zalman Schachter-Shalomi z"l)

On Purim

בִּימֵי מָרְדְּכַי וְאֶסְתֵּר בְּשׁוּשַׁן   Bimei Mordechai v'Ester b'Shushan

הַבִּירָה, כְּשֶׁעָמַד עֲלֵיהֶם   habirah, k'she·amad aleihem

הָמָן הָרָשָׁע, בִּקֵּשׁ לְהַשְׁמִיד, לַהֲרֹג   Haman harasha, bikeish l'hashmid, laharog

וּלְאַבֵּד אֶת כָּל הַיְּהוּדִים,   ulabeid et kol haihudim,

מִנַּעַר וְעַד זָקֵן, טַף וְנָשִׁים,   mina·ar v'ad zakein, taf v'nashim,

בְּיוֹם אֶחָד בִּשְׁלֹשָׁה עָשָׂר לְחֹדֶשׁ   b'yom echad bishlosha asar l'chodesh

שְׁנֵים עָשָׂר,   sh'neim asar,

הוּא חֹדֶשׁ אֲדָר, וּשְׁלָלָם לָבוֹז.   hu chodesh Adar, ushlalam lavoz.

וְאַתָּה בְּרַחֲמֶיךָ הָרַבִּים   V'atah b'rachamecha harabim

הֵפַרְתָּ אֶת עֲצָתוֹ,   heifarta et atzato,

וְקִלְקַלְתָּ אֶת מַחֲשַׁבְתּוֹ,   v'kilkalta et mach·shavto,

וַהֲשֵׁבוֹתָ לוֹ גְּמוּלוֹ בְּרֹאשׁוֹ.   vahasheivota lo g'mulo b'rosho.

In the days of Mordechai and Esther in Shushan, the capital,
when the wicked Haman arose before them and sought to destroy, to slay, and to
exterminate all the Jews — young and old, infants and women —
on the same day, the thirteenth of the twelfth month, which is the month of Adar,
and to plunder their possessions:
You, in Your abundant mercy,
nullified his counsel and frustrated his intention
and caused his design to return upon his own head.

וְעַל כֻּלָּם יִתְבָּרַךְ וְיִתְרוֹמַם   V'al kulam yitbarach v'yit·romam
שִׁמְךָ מַלְכֵּנוּ   shimcha Malkeinu
תָּמִיד לְעוֹלָם וָעֶד.   tamid l'olam va·ed,

For all these things, O God, let Your name forever be praised,

---

During the Ten Days of Repentance:

וּכְתֹב לְחַיִּים טוֹבִים כָּל בְּנֵי בְרִיתֶךָ   u'chtov l'chayim tovim kol b'nei v'ritecha

May all the children of Your covenant be inscribed for a life of goodness

---

וְכֹל הַחַיִּים יוֹדוּךָ סֶּלָה,   v'chol hachayim yoducha selah,
וִיהַלְלוּ אֶת שִׁמְךָ   vihal'lu et shimcha
בֶּאֱמֶת,   be·emet,
הָאֵל יְשׁוּעָתֵנוּ וְעֶזְרָתֵנוּ סֶלָה.   ha·El y'shu·ateinu v'ezrateinu selah.
בָּרוּךְ אַתָּה, יהוה,   Baruch atah, יהוה,
הַטּוֹב שִׁמְךָ וּלְךָ נָאֶה לְהוֹדוֹת.   hatov shimcha ulcha na·eh l'hodot.

for You are the God of our redemption and our hope.
Blessed are You, יהוה, whose Name is good
and who does great things worthy of our thanksgiving.

שָׁלוֹם רָב עַל יִשְׂרָאֵל עַמְּךָ   Shalom rav al Yisra·el am'cha
תָּשִׂים לְעוֹלָם,   tasim l'olam,
כִּי אַתָּה הוּא   ki atah hu
מֶלֶךְ אָדוֹן לְכָל הַשָּׁלוֹם.   melech adon l'chol hashalom.
וְטוֹב בְּעֵינֶיךָ לְבָרֵךְ   V'tov b'einecha l'vareich
אֶת עַמְּךָ יִשְׂרָאֵל   et am'cha Yisra·el
בְּכָל עֵת וּבְכָל שָׁעָה בִּשְׁלוֹמֶךָ.   b'chol eit uv'chol sha·ah bishlomecha.

Grant abundant peace to Your people Israel always,
for You are the Sovereign of all peace.
May it be pleasing in Your eyes
to bless Your people Israel
in every season and moment with Your peace.

During the Ten Days of Repentance:

בְּסֵפֶר חַיִּים, בְּרָכָה וְשָׁלוֹם,   B'sefer chayim, b'rachah, v'shalom,
וּפַרְנָסָה טוֹבָה, נִזָּכֵר וְנִכָּתֵב לְפָנֶיךָ,   ufarnasa tova, nizacheir v'nikateiv l'fanecha,
אֲנַחְנוּ וְכָל עַמְּךָ בֵּית יִשְׂרָאֵל,   anachnu v'chol am'cha beit Yisra·el,
לְחַיִּים טוֹבִים וּלְשָׁלוֹם.   l'chayim tovim ulshalom.

In the book of life, blessing, peace, and prosperity,
may we be remembered and inscribed by You,
— we and all Your people Israel —
for a good life and for peace.

בָּרוּךְ אַתָּה, יהוה, הַמְבָרֵךְ   Baruch atah, יהוה, ham'vareich
אֶת עַמּוֹ יִשְׂרָאֵל בַּשָּׁלוֹם.   et amo Yisra·el bashalom.

עֹשֶׂה שָׁלוֹם בִּמְרוֹמָיו,   Oseh shalom bimromav,
הוּא יַעֲשֶׂה שָׁלוֹם עָלֵינוּ   hu ya·aseh shalom aleinu
וְעַל כָּל יִשְׂרָאֵל,   v'al kol Yisra·el,
וְעַל כָּל יוֹשְׁבֵי תֵבֵל,   v'al kol yoshvei teiveil;
וְאִמְרוּ: אָמֵן.   v'imru: Amen.

May the One who makes peace in the heavens
make peace for us,
for all Israel,
and for all who dwell on earth.
And let us say: Amen.

Broken Open

When life is full of ease, spirituality is like cotton candy—fluffy, airy, and unserious....

And then something happens. Someone gets sick, or a relationship ends. Or a pet dies, or I lose my job. Or a friend dies unexpectedly.

And then we go searching for meaning. Not answers necessarily... but significance, meaning. Now the self-satisfied smirk of the critic melts into something less sure of itself. What can be understood in the midst of this tragedy, about the fragility of the human condition or the impossibility of holding onto it? And what are the forms which, over the years, people like me have created to contain this grief?

Thus pain becomes a gate to the recovery of the spiritual tones of living. I fail; I lose; and so I grow closer to the parts of myself which feel more authentic, more connected. Spiritual paths may not be as sophisticated or arch as other ways of being. They may be mocked in the pages of the *Times*. But at some point, most of us find ourselves broken—and hopefully broken open.

It's easy to be cynical about this sudden return to religious, spiritual, philosophical, or artistic homes long abandoned. We seem to be spiritual equivalents of fair-weather fans, clinging to a tradition or practice in our moment of need, then discarding it once again, when the moment of crisis has passed. Really, though, we are just flawed humans. To admit our inconsistency is only another necessary surrender. Fine, we are inconsistent. What do we sense to be true when we are at our weakest, our most open?

(Rabbi Jay Michaelson)

The Kaddish: A Door

The Kaddish which follows
—known as Kaddish Shaleim (whole Kaddish)—
is the doorway
between the Amidah
and our concluding prayers.

Where have tonight's prayers taken you?
Whatever you're feeling in this moment,
bring that into your prayer.

Kaddish Shaleim

יִתְגַּדַּל וְיִתְקַדַּשׁ שְׁמֵהּ רַבָּא,   Yitgadal v'yitkadash, sh'meih raba,
בְּעָלְמָא דִּי בְרָא כִרְעוּתֵהּ,   b'al'ma di v'ra chiruteih,
וְיַמְלִיךְ מַלְכוּתֵהּ   v'yamlich malchuteih
בְּחַיֵּיכוֹן וּבְיוֹמֵיכוֹן   b'chayeichon uvyomeichon
וּבְחַיֵּי דְכָל בֵּית יִשְׂרָאֵל.   uvchayei d'chol beit Yisra·el
בַּעֲגָלָא וּבִזְמַן קָרִיב.   ba·agala uvizman kariv.
וְאִמְרוּ: אָמֵן.   V'imru: Amen.

יְהֵא שְׁמֵהּ רַבָּא מְבָרַךְ   Y'hei sh'meih raba m'varach
לְעָלַם וּלְעָלְמֵי עָלְמַיָּא.   l'alam ulalmei almaya.

Magnified and sanctified! Magnified and sanctified!
May God's Great Name fill the world God created.
May God's splendor be seen in the world
in your life, in your days, in the life of all Israel.
Quickly and soon! And let us say, Amen.

Forever may the Great Name be blessed!

יִתְבָּרַךְ וְיִשְׁתַּבַּח,   Yitbarach v'yishtabach
וְיִתְפָּאַר וְיִתְרוֹמַם וְיִתְנַשֵּׂא   v'yitpa·ar v'yit·romam v'yitnasei
וְיִתְהַדָּר וְיִתְעַלֶּה וְיִתְהַלָּל   v'yit·hadar v'yitaleh v'yit·halal
שְׁמֵהּ דְּקֻדְשָׁא בְּרִיךְ הוּא   sh'meih d'kudsha b'rich hu
לְעֵלָּא   l'eila

During the Ten Days of Repentance:
וּלְעֵלָּא   uleila

מִכָּל בִּרְכָתָא וְשִׁירָתָא,   min kol birchata v'shirata,
תֻּשְׁבְּחָתָא וְנֶחֱמָתָא,   tushb'chata v'nechemata,
דַּאֲמִירָן בְּעָלְמָא,   da·amiran b'al'ma,
וְאִמְרוּ: אָמֵן.   v'imru: Amen.

Blessed and praised! Splendid and supreme!
May the holy name, Bless God, be praised,
beyond all the blessings and songs,
comforts and consolations,
that can be offered in this world.
And let us say: Amen.

תִּתְקַבֵּל צְלוֹתְהוֹן וּבָעוּתְהוֹן   Titkabal tz'lot'hon uva·ut'hon
דְּכָל (בֵּית) יִשְׂרָאֵל קֳדָם אֲבוּהוֹן   d'chol (beit) Yisra·el kodam avuhon
דִּי בִשְׁמַיָּא, וְאִמְרוּ: אָמֵן.   di vishmaya, v'imru: Amen.

יְהֵא שְׁלָמָא רַבָּא מִן שְׁמַיָּא   Y'hei sh'lama raba min sh'maya
וְחַיִּים עָלֵינוּ וְעַל כָּל יִשְׂרָאֵל,   v'chayim aleinu v'al kol Yisra·el;
וְאִמְרוּ: אָמֵן.   v'imru: Amen.

עֹשֶׂה שָׁלוֹם בִּמְרוֹמָיו   Oseh shalom bimromav,
הוּא יַעֲשֶׂה שָׁלוֹם   hu ya·aseh shalom,
עָלֵינוּ וְעַל כָּל יִשְׂרָאֵל,   aleinu v'al kol Yisra·el,
וְעַל כָּל יוֹשְׁבֵי תֵבֵל,   v'al kol yoshvei teiveil;
וְאִמְרוּ: אָמֵן.   v'imru: Amen.

May our prayers, and the prayers of the entire community,
be accepted before You, our Parent.

May there be peace and life, great peace and life
from heaven above
for us and all Israel.
And let us say, Amen!

May the One who makes peace in the high heavens
make peace for us,
for our whole community,
and for all the peoples of the world.
And let us say: Amen.

Psalm 23

מִזְמוֹר לְדָוִד,   Mizmor l'David.

יהוה רֹעִי, לֹא אֶחְסָר.   יהוה ro·i, lo echsar.

בִּנְאוֹת דֶּשֶׁא יַרְבִּיצֵנִי,   Binot desheh yarbitzeini,

עַל מֵי מְנֻחוֹת יְנַהֲלֵנִי.   al mei menuchot y'nahaleini.

נַפְשִׁי יְשׁוֹבֵב,   Nafshi y'shoveiv,

יַנְחֵנִי בְמַעְגְּלֵי צֶדֶק,   yancheini v'mag'lei tzedek,

לְמַעַן שְׁמוֹ.   lema·an sh'mo.

גַּם כִּי אֵלֵךְ בְּגֵיא צַלְמָוֶת,   Gam ki eilech b'gei tzalmavet,

לֹא אִירָא רָע כִּי אַתָּה עִמָּדִי,   lo ira ra, ki atah imadi,

שִׁבְטְךָ וּמִשְׁעַנְתֶּךָ,   shivt'cha umishantecha,

הֵמָּה יְנַחֲמֻנִי.   heima y'nachamuni.

תַּעֲרֹךְ לְפָנַי, שֻׁלְחָן נֶגֶד צֹרְרָי,   Ta·aroch lefanai, shulchan neged tzor'rai,

דִּשַּׁנְתָּ בַשֶּׁמֶן רֹאשִׁי,   dishanta vashemen roshi

כּוֹסִי רְוָיָה.   kosi r'vayah.

אַךְ טוֹב וָחֶסֶד יִרְדְּפוּנִי   Ach tov vachesed yird'funi

כָּל יְמֵי חַיָּי,   kol y'mei chayai,

וְשַׁבְתִּי בְּבֵית יהוה   v'shavti b'veit יהוה

לְאֹרֶךְ יָמִים.   l'orech yamim.

A psalm of David:
יהוה is my shepherd; I shall not want.
God makes me lie down in green pastures
and leads me beside still waters to restore my soul;
God leads me in paths of righteousness
for the sake of God's name.
Though I walk through the valley
of the shadow of death,
I shall fear no evil,
for You are with me;
Your rod and Your staff,
they comfort me.
You set a table before me in the presence of my enemies.
You anoint my head with oil;
my cup overflows.
Truly goodness and mercy will follow me
all the days of my life,
and I will dwell
in the house of יהוה forever.

Filled to Overflowing

The Holy one is my Guide;
    my life is whole.
We journey together
    over fertile hillsides
    and rest
    beside nourishing springs.
This is my spirit
    ever renewed,
    for my Guide leads me
    down paths of fullness.
Even when my steps lead
    into the kingdom of death
    I do not fear
    for I know you are with me.
Your presence
    your shelter
    is a comfort to me.
With you I can set myself aright
    in the face of
    deepest sorrow;
    and soon my joy is filled to overflowing.
As I journey on,
    nothing but kindness and love
    shall follow
    until the day I finally return.
To my Source,
    my destination.

(Rabbi Brant Rosen)

El Malei Rachamim: God of Compassion

אֵל מָלֵא רַחֲמִים, שׁוֹכֵן בַּמְּרוֹמִים,　　El malei rachamim, shochein bam'romim,
הַמְצֵא מְנוּחָה נְכוֹנָה　　hamtzei m'nuchah n'chonah
תַּחַת כַּנְפֵי הַשְּׁכִינָה,　　tachat kanfei hashechinah,
עִם קְדוֹשִׁים וּטְהוֹרִים　　im k'doshim ut·horim
כְּזֹהַר הָרָקִיעַ מַזְהִירִים,　　k'zohar haraki·a maz·hirim ,
＿＿＿＿＿＿＿＿ אֶת נִשְׁמַת　　et nishmat ＿＿＿＿＿＿＿＿

for a man say:

שֶׁהָלַךְ לְעוֹלָמוֹ　　shehalach l'olamo,
בְּגַן עֵדֶן תְּהֵא מְנוּחָתוֹ.　　b'gan Eden t'hei m'nucha·to.
אָנָּא בַּעַל הָרַחֲמִים יַסְתִּירֵהוּ　　Ana ba·al harachamim yastirei·hu
בְּסֵתֶר כְּנָפֶיךָ לְעוֹלָמִים,　　b'seiter k'nafecha l'olamim,
וְיִצְרֹר בִּצְרוֹר הַחַיִּים　　v'yitzror bitzror hachayim
אֶת נִשְׁמָתוֹ, יהוה הוּא נַחֲלָתוֹ,　　et nishmato. יהוה hu nachala·to.
וְיָנוּחַ בְּשָׁלוֹם עַל מִשְׁכָּבוֹ,　　v'yanu·ach b'shalom al mishkavo,
וְנֹאמַר אָמֵן.　　v'nomar amen.

for a woman say:

שֶׁהָלְכָה לְעוֹלָמָהּ　　shehal'chah l'olamah,
בְּגַן עֵדֶן תְּהֵא מְנוּחָתָהּ.　　b'gan Eden t'hei m'nucha·tah.
אָנָּא בַּעַל הָרַחֲמִים יַסְתִּירֶהָ　　Ana ba·al harachamim yastirehah
בְּסֵתֶר כְּנָפֶיךָ לְעוֹלָמִים,　　b'seiter k'nafecha l'olamim,
וְיִצְרֹר בִּצְרוֹר הַחַיִּים　　v'yitzror bitzror hachayim
אֶת נִשְׁמָתָהּ, יהוה הוּא נַחֲלָתָהּ,　　et nishmatah. יהוה hu nachalatah.
וְתָנוּחַ בְּשָׁלוֹם עַל מִשְׁכָּבָהּ,　　v'tanu·ach b'shalom al mishkavah,
וְנֹאמַר אָמֵן.　　v'nomar amen.

Compassionate God, Spirit of the universe,
Grant peace beneath the shelter of Your presence
among the holy and the pure
who shine with the splendor of the heavens,
to the soul of our dear one ＿＿＿＿＿＿
who has gone to their reward.
May the Garden of Eden be their rest.
O God of mercy,
guard them forever in the shadow of Your wings.
May their soul be bound up in the bond of life.
May they rest in peace.
And let us say: Amen.

Elah M'lei·at Rachamim

This version of El Malei Rachamim uses feminine Hebrew,
speaking to divinity in feminine form.

אֵלָה מְלֵאַת רַחֲמִים   Elah m'lei·at rachamim,

שׁוֹכֶנֶת בַּמְּרוֹמִים,   shochenet bam'romim,

הַמְצִיאִי מְנוּחָה נְכוֹנָה   hamtzi·i m'nuchah n'chonah

תַּחַת כַּנְפֵי הַשְּׁכִינָה   tachat kanfei hashechinah

בְּמַעֲלוֹת קְדוֹשׁוֹת וּטְהוֹרוֹת   b'ma·alot k'doshot ut·horot

כְּזֹהַר הָרָקִיעַ מַזְהִירוֹת   k'zohar haraki·a maz·hirot

אֶת נִשְׁמַת _____   et nishmat _____

שֶׁהָלְכָה לְעוֹלָמָהּ   shehal'chah l'olamah

בְּגַן עֵדֶן תְּהֵא מְנוּחָתָהּ.   b'Gan Eden t'hei m'nuchatah.

אָנָּא גְּבִירַת הָרַחֲמִים   Aana g'virat harachamim

תַּסְתִּירִיהָ בְּצֵל כְּנָפַיִךְ   tastirihah betzel k'nafayich

לְעוֹלָמִים, וְצִרְרִי בִּצְרוֹר הַחַיִּים   l'olamim, v'tzir'ri bitzror hachayim

אֶת נִשְׁמָתָהּ,   et nishmatah,

שְׁכִינָה הִיא נַחֲלָתָהּ   Shechinah hi nachalatah

וְתָנוּחַ בְּשָׁלוֹם עַל מִשְׁכָּבָהּ,   v'tanu·ach b'shalom al mishkavah,

וְנֹאמַר: אָמֵן.   v'nomar: Amen.

God filled with mercy,
dwelling in the heavens' heights,
bring proper rest
beneath the wings of your Shechinah,
amid the ranks of the holy and the pure
shining like the brilliance of the skies,
to the soul of our beloved _____
who has gone to her eternal place of rest.
May her rest be in the garden of Eden.
May you who are the source of mercy
shelter her beneath your wings eternally,
and weave her soul into the web of life
that she may rest in peace.
And let us say: Amen.

(Rabbi Jill Hammer)

Aleinu

Short Aleinu (Ein Od Mil'vado)

אֵין עוֹד מִלְבַדּוֹ,   Ein od mil'vado,

יהוה הוּא הָאֱלֹהִים.   יהוה hu ha·eohim.

There is nothing but God; God is God.

Aleinu (Full-Text)

עָלֵינוּ לְשַׁבֵּחַ לַאֲדוֹן הַכֹּל,   Aleinu l'shabei·ach la·adon hakol,

לָתֵת גְּדֻלָּה לְיוֹצֵר בְּרֵאשִׁית,   lateit g'dulah l'yotzeir b'reishit,

שֶׁלֹּא/שֶׁלּוֹ*   shelo

עָשָׂנוּ כְּגוֹיֵי הָאֲרָצוֹת   asanu k'goyei ha·aratzot,

וְלֹא/וְלוֹ* ,   v'lo

שָׂמָנוּ כְּמִשְׁפְּחוֹת הָאֲדָמָה,   samanu k'mishp'chot ha·adamah,

שֶׁלֹּא/שֶׁלּוֹ*   shelo

שָׂם חֶלְקֵנוּ כָּהֶם,   sam chelkeinu kahem,

וְגֹרָלֵנוּ כְּכָל הֲמוֹנָם.   v'goraleinu k'chol hamonam.

It is up to us to praise the Source of all, to exalt the Molder of creation.
We are:

made for God like all nations.	(or)	not made like other nations.

We are:

placed here for God like all humanity.	(or)	unlike other peoples.

Our portion and our fate are:

for God's own sake.	(or)	not like those of other peoples.

---

*Pray either לֹא, pronounced lo ("not"), or לוֹ, also pronounced lo ("for God"). The first articulates Jewish chosenness; the second, post-triumphalism.

וַאֲנַחְנוּ כּוֹרְעִים   Va·anachnu kor'im

וּמִשְׁתַּחֲוִים וּמוֹדִים,   umishtachavim umodim,

לִפְנֵי מֶלֶךְ,   lifnei melech

מַלְכֵי הַמְּלָכִים,   malchei ham'lachim,

הַקָּדוֹשׁ בָּרוּךְ הוּא.   hakadosh baruch hu.

We bow low and prostrate in thanks
before the Source of all sources,
the Holy One, blessed is God.

שֶׁהוּא נוֹטֶה שָׁמַיִם וְיֹסֵד אָרֶץ,   Shehu noteh shamayim v'yoseid aretz,

וּמוֹשַׁב יְקָרוֹ בַּשָּׁמַיִם מִמַּעַל,   umoshav y'karo bashamayim mima·al,

וּשְׁכִינַת עֻזּוֹ בְּגָבְהֵי מְרוֹמִים.   ush·chinat uzo b'govhei m'romim.

הוּא אֱלֹהֵינוּ, אֵין עוֹד.   Hu Eloheinu, ein od.

God sets out the heavens and establishes the earth.
God's honored place is in the heights of our aspirations;
God's powerful presence is in the heavens of our hopes.
This is our God; there is none else.

אֱמֶת מַלְכֵּנוּ אֶפֶס זוּלָתוֹ.   Emet malkeinu efes zulato.

כַּכָּתוּב בְּתוֹרָתוֹ: וְיָדַעְתָּ הַיּוֹם   Kakatuv b'torato: V'yadata hayom

וַהֲשֵׁבֹתָ אֶל לְבָבֶךָ,   vahasheivota el l'vavecha,

כִּי יהוה הוּא הָאֱלֹהִים בַּשָּׁמַיִם   ki יהוה hu ha·elohim bashamayim

מִמַּעַל, וְעַל הָאָרֶץ מִתָּחַת, אֵין עוֹד.   mima·al, v'al ha·aretz mitachat, ein od.

There is nothing that God is not.
As it is written in God's sacred teaching:
"You shall know this day
and place upon your heart
that יהוה is God in heaven above and earth below;
there is none else."

עַל כֵּן נְקַוֶּה לְּךָ יהוה אֱלֹהֵינוּ,   Al kein n'kaveh l'cha יהוה Eloheinu,

לִרְאוֹת מְהֵרָה בְּתִפְאֶרֶת עֻזֶּךָ,   lirot m'heirah b'tiferet uzecha,

לְהַעֲבִיר גִּלּוּלִים מִן הָאָרֶץ   l'ha·avir gilulim min ha·aretz,

וְהָאֱלִילִים כָּרוֹת יִכָּרֵתוּן,   v'ha·elilim karot yikareitun,

לְתַקֵּן עוֹלָם בְּמַלְכוּת שַׁדַּי.   l'takein olam b'malchut Shaddai.

וְכָל בְּנֵי בָשָׂר יִקְרְאוּ בִשְׁמֶךָ,
לְהַפְנוֹת אֵלֶיךָ כָּל רִשְׁעֵי אָרֶץ.
יַכִּירוּ וְיֵדְעוּ כָּל יוֹשְׁבֵי תֵבֵל,
כִּי לְךָ תִּכְרַע כָּל בֶּרֶךְ
תִּשָּׁבַע כָּל לָשׁוֹן.

V'chol b'nei vasar yikr'u vishmecha,
l'hafnot eilecha kol rishei aretz.
Yakiru v'yeid'u kol yosh'vei teiveil
ki l'cha tichra kol berech
tishava kol lashon.

Therefore we hope in You, יהוה our God. May we soon see the power of
Your beauty wipe away false gods from the earth and sweep away idolatry,
so that the truth of Your sovereign presence will repair the world.
Then will all humanity call Your name,
and then all that had been dark will turn to Your light.
All who dwell on earth will feel in their hearts and know in their minds
that You are our source—the true object of devotion and loyalty.

לְפָנֶיךָ יהוה אֱלֹהֵינוּ יִכְרְעוּ וְיִפֹּלוּ,
וְלִכְבוֹד שִׁמְךָ יְקָר יִתֵּנוּ.
וִיקַבְּלוּ כֻלָּם אֶת עוֹל מַלְכוּתֶךָ.
וְתִמְלֹךְ עֲלֵיהֶם מְהֵרָה לְעוֹלָם וָעֶד.
כִּי הַמַּלְכוּת שֶׁלְּךָ הִיא,
וּלְעוֹלְמֵי עַד תִּמְלוֹךְ בְּכָבוֹד.

L'fanecha יהוה Eloheinu yichr'u v'yipolu,
v'lichvod shimcha y'kar yiteinu.
Vikab'lu chulam et ol malchutecha.
V'timloch aleihem m'heirah l'olam va·ed.
Ki hamalchut shel'cha hi,
ulol'mei ad timloch b'chavod.

Before You, יהוה our God, will they bend low
and pay homage to glorify Your name.
Then all will accept the obligations of living in Your world—
obligations of hope, love and duty to heaven and humanity.
Then You will surely rule forever and ever.
For the earth is Yours, and Your glory fills it forever.

כַּכָּתוּב בְּתוֹרָתֶךָ:
יהוה יִמְלֹךְ לְעוֹלָם וָעֶד.
וְנֶאֱמַר:
וְהָיָה יהוה לְמֶלֶךְ
עַל כָּל הָאָרֶץ,
בַּיּוֹם הַהוּא יִהְיֶה יהוה אֶחָד,
וּשְׁמוֹ אֶחָד.

Kakatuv b'toratecha:
יהוה yimloch l'olam va·ed.
V'ne·emar:
v'hayah יהוה lemelech
al kol ha·aretz,
bayom hahu yihyeh יהוה echad,
ushmo echad.

Then shall Your realm be established on earth,
and the word of Your prophet fulfilled:
"Adonai will reign forever and ever.
On that day, יהוה shall be One, and God's name shall be One."

Mourner's Kaddish

יִתְגַּדַּל וְיִתְקַדַּשׁ שְׁמֵהּ רַבָּא,
בְּעָלְמָא דִּי בְרָא כִרְעוּתֵהּ,
וְיַמְלִיךְ מַלְכוּתֵהּ
בְּחַיֵּיכוֹן וּבְיוֹמֵיכוֹן
וּבְחַיֵּי דְכָל בֵּית יִשְׂרָאֵל,
בַּעֲגָלָא וּבִזְמַן קָרִיב,
וְאִמְרוּ: אָמֵן.

Yitgadal v'yitkadash, sh'meih raba,
b'al'ma di v'ra chiruteih,
v'yamlich malchuteih
b'chayeichon uvyomeichon
uvchayei d'chol beit Yisra·el,
ba·agala uvizman kariv,
v'imru: **Amen.**

יְהֵא שְׁמֵהּ רַבָּא מְבָרַךְ
לְעָלַם וּלְעָלְמֵי עָלְמַיָּא.

Y'hei sh'mei raba m'varach
l'alam ulal'mei al'maya.

יִתְבָּרַךְ וְיִשְׁתַּבַּח, וְיִתְפָּאַר
וְיִתְרוֹמַם וְיִתְנַשֵּׂא וְיִתְהַדָּר וְיִתְעַלֶּה
וְיִתְהַלָּל שְׁמֵהּ דְּקֻדְשָׁא
בְּרִיךְ הוּא
לְעֵלָּא

Yitbarach v'yishtabach v'yitpa·ar
v'yit·romam v'yitnasei v'yit·hadar v'yitaleh
v'yit·halal sh'meih d'kudsha
b'rich hu
l'eila

During the Ten Days of Repentance:
וּלְעֵלָּא

uleila

מִן כָּל בִּרְכָתָא וְשִׁירָתָא,
תֻּשְׁבְּחָתָא וְנֶחֱמָתָא,
דַּאֲמִירָן בְּעָלְמָא, וְאִמְרוּ: **אָמֵן.**

min kol birchata v'shirata,
tushb'chata v'nechemata,
da·amiran b'al'ma, v'imru: Amen.

יְהֵא שְׁלָמָא רַבָּא מִן שְׁמַיָּא
וְחַיִּים עָלֵינוּ וְעַל כָּל יִשְׂרָאֵל,
וְאִמְרוּ: אָמֵן.
עֹשֶׂה שָׁלוֹם בִּמְרוֹמָיו
הוּא יַעֲשֶׂה שָׁלוֹם עָלֵינוּ
וְעַל כָּל יִשְׂרָאֵל,
וְעַל כָּל יוֹשְׁבֵי תֵבֵל,
וְאִמְרוּ: **אָמֵן.**

Y'hei sh'lama raba min sh'maya
v'chayim aleinu v'al kol Yisra·el,
v'imru: Amen.
Oseh shalom bimromav,
hu ya·aseh shalom, aleinu
v'al kol Yisra·el,
v'al kol yosh'vei teiveil,
v'imru: **Amen.**

I pray to You God,
that the power residing in Your Great Name
be increased and made sacred
in this world which God created freely
in order to preside in it, and grow its freeing power
and bring about the messianic era.
May this happen during our lifetime
and during the lifetime of all of us
living now, the house of Israel.
May this happen soon, without delay
and by saying AMEN we express agreement and hope, AMEN.

May that immense power residing in God's great name
flow freely into our world and worlds beyond.

May that Great Name, that sacred energy,
be shaped
and made effective
and be acknowledged
and be given the right honor
and be seen as beautiful
and uplifting
and bring jubilation.
Way beyond our input
of worshipful song and praise
which we express in this world
as our agreement and hope, AMEN.

May that endless peace
that heaven can release for us
bring about the good life
for us and for all Israel
as we express our agreement and hope, AMEN.

You, who harmonize it all
on the highest planes:
bring harmony and peace to us,
to all Israel and all sentient beings
as we express our agreement and hope, AMEN.

(translation: Rabbi Zalman Shachter-Shalomi z"l)

*(Each time Mourner's Kaddish appears in this volume,
it is translated by someone different.
Each translation is unique, and each evokes
a particular quality of the original Aramaic.)*

Mourner's Kaddish Poem

So often am I lost, yet through the pall, yet through the tarnish, show me the way back, through my betrayals, my dismay, my heart's leak, my mind's sway, eyes' broken glow, groan of the soul—which convey all that isn't real, for every soul to These Hands careen. And let us say, Amen.

Say you will show me the way back, my Rock, my Alarm. Lead the way, Oh my Yah.

And yet in shock and yet in shame and yet in awe and yet to roam and yet to stay and yet right here and yet away and yet —"Halleluyah!" my heartbeat speaks, for You live in all this murk and too in the clear and too in our wreckage. You are the mirror of our souls, let us say: Amen

Life may harm me, rob me, ream me raw, try me, even slay me. Over all You will prevail. And let us say: Amen

Say You shall loan me a tomorrow, say You shall loan another day to all who are called Yisra·el and all called Yish'mael and all called We and They, and let us say, Amen.

(Elliot bat Tzedek)

The Angel Song (from the Bedtime Sh'ma)

This song, which describes and evokes four angelic presences surrounding us as we approach sleep, comes from the traditional liturgy of the bedtime Sh'ma.

בְּשֵׁם יהוה אֱלֹהֵי יִשְׂרָאֵל,	B'sheim יהוה, Elohei Yisra·el
מִימִינִי מִיכָאֵל,	mimini Micha·el,
וּמִשְׂמֹאלִי גַבְרִיאֵל,	umis'moli Gavri·el,
וּמִלְּפָנַי אוּרִיאֵל,	umil'fanai Uri·el,
וּמֵאֲחוֹרַי רְפָאֵל,	umei·achorai R'fa·el,
וְעַל רֹאשִׁי וּמֵעַל תַּחְתִּי	v'al roshi, umei·al tachtai,
שְׁכִינַת אֵל.	Shechinat El.

In the name of God, the God of Israel:
On my right is Michael, on my left is Gavriel.
In front of me is Uriel, behind me Raphael.
And all above, surrounding me, Shechinat-El.

The four angels who watch over us as we sleep:

Micha-el: Who is Like You, God? (Wonder)
Gavri-el: God's Strength (Strength)
Uri-el: God's Light (Light)
Rapha-el: God's Healing (Comfort)

After *Shiva*

Prayer for When a Holiday Cancels *Shiva*

O God, at sundown my formal mourning
is meant to end, but I'm not ready.
My heart is still tender. I still need
to be cradled. How will I shift gears
from sorrow to rejoicing?

I don't feel ready for this holiday.
I'm dislocated in spirit and in time.
Be with me as my boat drifts on these currents.
Help me trust that I'm not alone,
that I will find my way to a familiar shore.

Don't ask me, God, to pretend away my grief.
Guide my loved ones to accompany me
wherever my heart needs to be.
And if I reach joy, to my own surprise,
protect me from guilt sparked by my rejoicing.

In years to come when this *yahrzeit* bumps again
into this holiday, grant me peace
as I stumble through the collision.
Let me be present to my heart, now
and always. Blessed are You, Who hears prayer.

(Rabbi Rachel Barenblat)

From *Shiva* to *Sh'loshim*

So you're approaching the end of *shiva*. That first week of mourning after the funeral, after the first Mourner's Kaddish, after the unthinkable act of shoveling a spadeful of earth and hearing it thud on unvarnished wood. *Shiva* means seven, the number of days of this first stage of grieving. One week: the most basic unit of Jewish time. After those seven days, a mourner enters the stage called *sh'loshim*, "thirty," which lasts through the first month after burial. But what does entering into *sh'loshim* mean? How does it, might it, have an impact on your life?

In the tangible world, the move from *shiva* to *sh'loshim* can have palpable implications. Traditional Jewish practice places a variety of restrictions on mourners during *shiva*—for instance: not wearing leather shoes, sitting on the ground or on a low stool (closeness to the earth is a sign of humility and mourning), not going to work, not engaging in physical intimacy. All of these restrictions are lifted during *sh'loshim*.

For contemporary liberal Jews who do not consider themselves bound by traditional *halakhot* (laws / ways-of-walking), the restrictions and their abeyance may or may not have meaning. You may not have given up leather or sex or anointing yourself with perfume or listening to music this week. But the psycho-spiritual shift of moving from *shiva* to *sh'loshim* is still significant. The shift from *shiva* to *sh'loshim* is all about expansion.

During the first week of mourning one's life may contract to a very small space. Perhaps you haven't left the *shiva* house at all. Or even if you've gone in and out of your home, you may have felt constricted, your life seemingly shrunken. Once *shiva* has ended, it is time to start expanding again. Open yourself to seeing more people. Allow yourself to immerse in your work life again. Expand your self-perception: you are not only a mourner, not only someone who grieves, but also someone who lives, works, struggles, and loves.

This may feel impossible. If it does, that's okay. Just know that our tradition believes that it is good for a mourner to try to open themselves to life again after that first, most-intense week of grief. Your sorrow may ebb and flow. You may experience times when you think you're close to okay again, and times when the floodwaters of emotion threaten to swamp you. Keep breathing. The emotional roller coaster is normal. You won't always feel this way, but—as the saying goes—the only way out is through.

If you've been burning a *shiva* candle all week, your candle will naturally flicker and gutter and run out of fuel as the week of *shiva* ends. (The candle is designed to last for seven days; that's what makes it a *shiva* candle.) When the candle extinguishes itself, that may feel like another blow, another loss. Remember that the candle is only a candle: a symbol of your mourning, but not a barometer of your spiritual state or of your loved one's presence.

You can still talk to your loved one, if there is meaning for you in that practice. You can talk to God. You can pray or meditate or sit in your silent car and wail— however you can best express whatever you're feeling. You might try writing a letter to your loved one at the end of *shiva*, telling them where you are and how you are as the first week of active mourning comes to its end. (What you do with the letter is up to you: save it? burn it? shred it and use the paper to mulch a new tree?)

Above all, be kind to yourself. Pay attention to what your heart needs.

This second stage of mourning lasts for one month, the time it takes for the moon to wax and become full and then wane again. This is an organic cycle, a mode of measuring time through observing the ebb and flow of the natural world. Just as the moon grows and shrinks, so our spirits and our hearts experience times of fullness and times of contraction. The end of *sh'loshim* is a time to begin looking toward fullness again. We trust that after the moon has disappeared, she will return; we trust that after our lives have been diminished by loss, light and meaning will flow into them again.

If you are moving from *shiva* into *sh'loshim*, or out of *sh'loshim* into the rest of the year: may the transition be what you need it to be. May this ancient way of thinking about mourning and the passage of time be meaningful for you; may time soothe your grief. One traditional practice is to mark the end of *shiva* by going for a walk around the block — a symbolic step out of the closeness of your home, into the wide world around you.

May the Source of Mercy bring you comfort along with all who mourn.

Prayers for the End of *Sh'loshim*

Upon Dismantling the House

Eileh Had'varim / These Are the Things.

Dear One, I look around me at what you left behind in this physical world and I am overwhelmed. I see a home that did not know you wouldn't return, and its bewilderment matches my own.

I collect up the bank statements and junk mail and utility bills. A cry of anguish issues from my pen each time I write the word "deceased" on an envelope. My voice catches with every phone call to close an account, my most intimate grief playing out in conversation with customer service.

I consider the clothes and housewares and furniture. Some will become souvenirs for me or for others—the items that evoke the happiest memories: you at your most elegant, you at your most characteristic. Other things will find shelter in thrift shops and charities, so that the artifacts of your life may bless strangers' lives as your love has blessed mine.

I may find words or objects you'd meant to keep private. I will do my best to respect your privacy. And may I be blessed that what I do learn might bring me a fuller understanding of who you were. Whatever I find, I will not stand in judgment. Each of us is a mix of concealed and revealed, and I would not expect otherwise of you.

I will find the souvenirs you saved. From childhood, from others' childhoods, from your life as lived: mementos, scrapbooks, photos, special trinkets. We who loved you will take some of these into our homes and lives and legacies. But there is too much for us to hold! You saved these things so they could each be looked at and appreciated one more time. And we will do that for you. We will look at each, and we will marvel and discuss and laugh and cry. We will snap pictures of them. And then we will let them go, releasing your attachments and fondnesses into the divine spheres, with our blessing.

May your soul be at ease, knowing that this work is not a burden but a privilege. I sew up these details with love. I hold these things in my hands, and that feels something like touching you. And in this way, our journey together continues, though worlds now lie between us.

May I be strong enough to carry the weight of this work. And gentle enough to feel its holiness. And as we who are left behind look and sort and smile and let go, may your Soul be unburdened and carried aloft.

(Irwin Keller)

When Will I Be Myself Again?

"When will I be myself again?"
Some Tuesday, perhaps,
In the late afternoon,
Sitting quietly with a cup of tea
And a cookie;
Or Wednesday, same time or later,
You will stir from a nap and see her;
You will pick up the phone to call her;
You will hear her voice – unexpected advice –
And maybe argue.
And you will not be frightened,
And you will not be sad,
And you will not be alone,
Not alone at all,
And your tears will warm you.
But not today,
And not tomorrow,
And not tomorrow's tomorrow,
But someday,
Some Tuesday, late in the afternoon,
Sitting quietly with a cup of tea
And a cookie
And you will be yourself again.

(Rabbi Lewis Eron)

Dinner Alone (After the Death of a Spouse)

Sitting alone now
eating dinner:
tempted by the simplicity
of an easy yogurt
the speed of a
bowl of cereal.

Fighting it alone now!
Chop, slice, dice, sauté.
I learned to cook to please him,
laying my culinary soul at his fork
sweetly blessed
by a clean plate and a kiss.

Moving ahead alone now
through an odd, disorienting light,
a partial eclipse of my being,
towards an unknown destination.
Pieces of my broken life
falling at my feet.

Repair this alone now.
Learn to use tools,
new tools, power tools —
any tool, really.
It would please him...
the repairs and a successful journey.

(Helene Armet)

Mourning to Dancing

What does it take to turn mourning to dancing?

First, a reaching forward.
A subtle movement out of the slump of our *shiva* chair.

Then, the planting of our feet on the ground.
"Yes," we are here and grounded in the roots of divine justice.
It is now possible to stand.

Though the whispers of fate and even the Angel of Death
Tell us to stay a while.
To reject words of consolation for the heaviness of our sorrow.
Though they would have us look away from ourselves and all life,
We face the dark.

And somewhere, a prism of light forms.
We can barely make it out.
But when our vision and we, too, are ready
We see it as bright as day:

"Arise."

Arise in the presence of friends.
Arise and leave behind the tear and the tearing.
Arise and make those first few steps among the living.

And though we stand up and sit down,
Agonize over what we are able to do and not do,
Individual acts of mind, body, and soul
Will lead us to give up the grief and ignite our dry bones.

And one of these days when we least expect it, we will find ourselves dancing.

(Devon Spier)

Ritual for the End of *Sh'loshim*

Optional: begin by blessing a glass of grape juice or wine.

I bless the fruit of the vine as an invitation to myself to relearn how to experience joy:

בָּרוּךְ אַתָּה, יהוה,   Baruch atah, יהוה,
אֱלֹהֵינוּ, מֶלֶךְ הָעוֹלָם,   Eloheinu, melech haolam,
בּוֹרֵא פְּרִי הַגָּפֶן.   borei p'ri hagafen.

A Fountain of Blessing are You,
יהוה, our God, sovereign of all space and time,
creator of the fruit of the vine.

* * *

Some end sh'loshim by pounding a nail into a board. An act of building, to symbolize that the mourner is ready to begin to build the next chapter of their life. A bang, to wake the mourner from their mourning sleep.

Some end sh'loshim by walking out of the house, around the block, and then back into the house through a different door. During the first month, life contracts. It is time now to take up more space in the world once again.

Some end sh'loshim with a shave or a haircut. An act of personal care; a symbolic return to paying attention to one's appearance once again, or a renewed commitment to being in one's body and experiencing pleasure again.

As I end *sh'loshim*, may my hands be graced with strength and skill as I begin to build my life anew.

As I end *sh'loshim*, may my feet be steady and sure as I begin to walk in the world again.

As I end *sh'loshim*, may I relearn how to take care of myself and how to feel sweetness in all four worlds of body, heart, mind, and spirit.

May my immersion in living waters cleanse me of the last month's grief, and allow me to emerge reborn and ready to begin again.

If no mikveh or source of "living waters" (such as a pond or lake) is available, a hot shower will do: it's not purifying according to halakha / Jewish law, but it can have a psycho-spiritual impact, especially if entered-into with the intention of washing away grief and emerging into new life.

Prayers for the End of the First Year

Prayer Before the Final Kaddish of the First Year

It is customary to recite Kaddish for a parent for eleven months. This prayer was written to recite before the final Kaddish. It was written for the author's mother, but could be recited for a parent or loved one of any gender.

Today is the last day I am saying Kaddish for you during this precious eleven-month journey of mourning and healing. You will always be my mother and I will always remember you in your wholeness, in this life and in the world to come.

You no longer need the first year's Kaddish to ascend to the place of true rest.

You are now in direct connection with Sh'meih Raba, the Great Name, the name that holds all of life and all of death, all of time and space. You are in the place of complete forgiveness, healing, and the deepest of shalom. You are in the womb of our Creation, under the wings and embrace of Shechinah herself.

Now you can watch over me. Help me ascend to my highest self, like you did when I was a child.

You will always be my mother and I will always remember you in your wholeness in this life and in the world to come.

(Rabbi Chaya Gusfield)

B'al'ma Di V'ra, or, Kaddish For My Father

The words go through my feet
into the ground, where they find the light
of my father: the peas
he planted and the grass he mowed,
the stray sticks he tossed into the woods
to keep the land clean,
and the logs he spun into candlesticks
for my table,
the good water he drew
from his well, the sand castles
he patiently dripped out of wet sand,
his black curls, his gray curls
as years passed, the kindness
with which he held my hand
at the beach and the hardware store,
the quiet joy with which he answered the phone,
the voice as strong and humble as soil,
the wisdom he shared about trees
and houses and the sea.

All the days he lived
are now stored in the earth.
When I say Kaddish,
all this comes into me
through the soles of my feet
and I feel his life
sowing itself in me,
a world-life
that never dies.

Then I send through my feet
my own life to greet his
to sow itself in him
because we love one another

and though I am alive and he is dead
we are still growing one world together.
We cannot be separated,
even by death,
even by life.

(Rabbi Jill Hammer)

A Mourner's Prayer

How fortunate to buy a white candle,
to know when to strike the match,
shovel dirt and hear it thud
on the lid, to reminisce
over photographs (to have photographs)
and fold his clothes for those less fortunate.

How luxurious to say Kaddish for one person,
letting grief resonate, deep bell tone
thrumming deeper and round.

O Love, reverberate, ricochet.
Loss and longing, lash out.

    She knows precisely who
she weeps for, leaving a stone on his stone
near the stone his father and mother share.

Welcome, Grief,
resident alien, baruch haba.
                Memory
will count Father in the minyan
of a daughter's heart.
                     Year after year
how privileged to light the candle.
    Most fortunate daughter thanks her father,
tear after tear.

(Maxine Silverman)

Cold Solace

When my mother died,
one of her honey cakes remained in the freezer.
I couldn't bear to see it vanish,
so it waited, pardoned,
in its ice cave behind the metal trays
for two more years.

On my forty-first birthday
I chipped it out,
a rectangular resurrection,
hefted the dead weight in my palm.
Before it thawed,
I sawed, with serrated knife,
the thinnest of slices —
Jewish Eucharist.

The amber squares
with their translucent panes of walnuts
tasted — even toasted — of freezer,
of frost,
a raisined delicacy delivered up
from a deli in the underworld.

I yearned to recall life, not death —
the still body in her pink nightgown on the bed,
how I lay in the shallow cradle of the scattered sheets
after they took it away,
inhaling her scent one last time.

I close my eyes, savor a wafer of
sacred cake on my tongue and
try to taste my mother, to discern
the message she baked in these loaves
when she was too ill to eat them:

I love you.
It will end.
Leave something of sweetness
and substance
in the mouth of the world.

(Anna Belle Kaufman)

Yahrzeit / Yizkor

The anniversary of a death is known as the yahrzeit. On a yahrzeit, you might choose to light a candle, say prayers of remembrance, and seek a minyan to say Kaddish in community.

Yizkor is the name given to the service of memorial prayers recited in community four times each year: at Pesach, at Shavuot, on Yom Kippur, and on Shemini Atzeret.

The heart of the Yizkor service is a series of silent prayers of remembrance, each geared toward a particular kind of relationship (parent, spouse, friend, etc.).

Yahrzeit

She lights a candle in a jar. He puts
it on the mantle. The candle burns because
it's the custom and their grief doesn't know
where to put itself. It might as well burn
inside a jar as anywhere on the earth.
There are heavens where the dead relive life
and hells where they do the same. But they light
a candle and watch it burn. It is so slow
like a light put down a well, canceled
by darkness the deeper it goes, like a body
fading in a hole, the day giving up its light.
The faintest glow casts a fainter shadow.
They follow that shadow across the ceiling
all afternoon and into the evening.
Maybe then it's time to say a prayer.
When she lights the candle his wife cries.
It's the custom. They don't believe. Despair
would tell them to do nothing, but that's no good.
They do what they can. They did what they could.

(Rodger Kamenetz)

Silent Prayers of Remembrance

In memory of a father:

יִזְכֹּר אֱלֹהִים נִשְׁמַת אָבִי מוֹרִי...   Yizkor Elohim nishmat avi mori…
שֶׁהָלַךְ לְעוֹלָמוֹ,   shehalach l'olamo,
בַּעֲבוּר שֶׁבְּלִי נֶדֶר אֶתֵּן צְדָקָה בַּעֲדוֹ.   ba·avur sheb'li neder etein tz'dakah ba·ado.
בִּשְׂכַר זֶה, תְּהֵא נַפְשׁוֹ צְרוּרָה   Bis·char zeh, t'hei nafsho tz'rurah
בִּצְרוֹר הַחַיִּים עִם נִשְׁמוֹת   bitzror hachayim im nishmot
אַבְרָהָם, יִצְחָק, וְיַעֲקֹב,   Avraham, Yitzchak, v'Ya·akov,
שָׂרָה, רִבְקָה, רָחֵל, וְלֵאָה,   Sarah, Rivkah, Racheil, v'Le·ah,
וְעִם שְׁאָר צַדִּיקִים וְצִדְקָנִיּוֹת   v'im sh'ar tzadikim v'tzidkaniyot
שֶׁבְּגַן עֵדֶן, וְנֹאמַר: אָמֵן.   sheb'Gan Eiden, v'nomar: Amen.

May God remember the soul of my father,
who has gone to his eternal reward.
I pledge acts of justice and charity in his memory.
May his soul be bound in the bonds of eternal life
along with the souls of our ancestors,
Avraham, Yitzchak, Ya·akov, Sarah, Rivkah, Rachel, and Leah.
May he rest in the perfect joy of Your presence. Amen.

In memory of a mother:

יִזְכֹּר אֱלֹהִים נִשְׁמַת אִמִּי מוֹרָתִי ...   Yizkor Elohim nishmat imi morati…
שֶׁהָלְכָה לְעוֹלָמָהּ,   shehal'chah l'olamah,
בַּעֲבוּר שֶׁבְּלִי נֶדֶר אֶתֵּן צְדָקָה בַּעֲדָהּ.   ba·avur sheb'li neder etein tz'dakah ba·adah.
בִּשְׂכַר זֶה, תְּהֵא נַפְשָׁהּ צְרוּרָה   Bis·char zeh, t'hei nafshah tz'rurah
בִּצְרוֹר הַחַיִּים עִם נִשְׁמוֹת   bitzror hachayim im nishmot
אַבְרָהָם, יִצְחָק, וְיַעֲקֹב,   Avraham, Yitzchak, v'Ya·akov,
שָׂרָה, רִבְקָה, רָחֵל, וְלֵאָה,   Sarah, Rivkah, Racheil v'Le·ah,
וְעִם שְׁאָר צַדִּיקִים וְצִדְקָנִיּוֹת   v'im sh'ar tzadikim v'tzidkaniyot
שֶׁבְּגַן עֵדֶן, וְנֹאמַר: אָמֵן.   sheb'Gan Eden, v'nomar: Amen.

May God remember the soul of my mother,
who has gone to her eternal reward.
I pledge acts of justice and charity in her memory.
May her soul be bound in the bonds of eternal life
along with the souls of our ancestors, Avraham, Yitzchak, Ya'akov, Sarah, Rivkah,
Rachel, and Leah. May she rest in the perfect joy of Your presence. Amen.

In memory of a hurtful parent:

O God: You know my heart. Indeed, You know me better than I know myself.
My emotions swirl as I say this prayer. The parent I remember was not kind
to me. His/her death left me with a legacy of unhealed wounds, of anger, and of
dismay that a parent could hurt a child as I was hurt.

Help me, O God, to subdue bitter emotions that do me no good, and to find that
place in myself where happier memories may lie hidden and where grief for all that
could have been, all that should have been, may be calmed by forgiveness, or at least
soothed by the passage of time.

I pray that You, who raise up slaves to freedom, will liberate me from the
oppression of my hurt and anger, and that You will lead me from this desert to Your
holy place.

(Rabbi Robert Saks)

In memory of a husband:

יִזְכּוֹר אֱלֹהִים Yizkor Elohim
נִשְׁמַת בַּעֲלִי הַיָּקָר... nishmat ba·ali hayakar...
שֶׁהָלַךְ לְעוֹלָמוֹ, she'halach l'olamo,
בַּעֲבוּר שֶׁבְּלִי נֶדֶר baavur sheb'li neder
אֶתֵּן צְדָקָה בַּעֲדוֹ. etein tz'dakah baado.
בִּשְׂכַר זֶה, תְּהֵא נַפְשׁוֹ צְרוּרָה Bis·char zeh, t'hei nafsho tz'rurah
בִּצְרוֹר הַחַיִּים עִם נִשְׁמוֹת bitzror hachayim im nishmot
אַבְרָהָם, יִצְחָק, וְיַעֲקֹב, Avraham, Yitzchak, v'Ya·akov;
שָׂרָה, רִבְקָה, רָחֵל, וְלֵאָה, Sarah, Rivkah, Racheil, v'Le·ah;
וְעִם שְׁאָר צַדִּיקִים וְצִדְקָנִיּוֹת v'im sh'ar tzadikim v'tzidkaniyot
שֶׁבְּגַן עֵדֶן, וְנֹאמַר: אָמֵן. sheb'Gan Eiden, v'nomar: Amen.

May God remember the soul of my husband,
who has gone to his eternal reward.
May his soul be bound in the bonds of eternal life
along with the souls of our ancestors,
Avraham, Yitzchak, Ya'akov, Sarah, Rivkah, Rachel, and Leah.
May he rest in the perfect joy of Your presence. Amen.

In memory of a wife:

יִזְכּוֹר אֱלֹהִים Yizkor Elohim
נִשְׁמַת אִשְׁתִּי הַיְקָרָה... nishmat ishti hay'karah…
שֶׁהָלְכָה לְעוֹלָמָהּ, shehal'chah l'olamah,
בַּעֲבוּר שֶׁבְּלִי נֶדֶר ba·avur sheb'li neder
אֶתֵּן צְדָקָה בַּעֲדָהּ. etein tz'dakah ba·adah.
בִּשְׂכַר זֶה, תְּהֵא נַפְשָׁהּ צְרוּרָה Bis·char zeh, t'hei nafshah tz'rurah
בִּצְרוֹר הַחַיִּים עִם נִשְׁמוֹת bitzror hachayim im nishmot
אַבְרָהָם, יִצְחָק, וְיַעֲקֹב, Avraham, Yitzchak, v'Ya·akov,
שָׂרָה, רִבְקָה, רָחֵל, וְלֵאָה, Sarah, Rivkah, Racheil v'Lei·ah,
וְעִם שְׁאָר צַדִּיקִים וְצִדְקָנִיּוֹת v'im sh'ar tzadikim v'tzidkaniyot
שֶׁבְּגַן עֵדֶן, וְנֹאמַר: אָמֵן. sheb'Gan Eden, v'nomar: Amen.

May God remember the soul of my wife
who has gone to her eternal reward.
May her soul be bound in the bonds of eternal life
along with the souls of our ancestors
Avraham, Yitzchak, and Ya'akov, Sarah, Rebecca, Rachel, and Leah.
May she rest satisfied in the perfect joy of Your presence. Amen.

In memory of a son:

יִזְכּוֹר אֱלֹהִים נִשְׁמַת Yizkor Elohim nishmat
בְּנִי הָאָהוּב... b'ni haahuv…
מַחְמַד עֵינַי שֶׁהָלַךְ לְעוֹלָמוֹ, machmad einai shehalach l'olamo.
אָנָּא תְּהֵא נַפְשׁוֹ צְרוּרָה Ana t'hei nafsho tz'rurah
בִּצְרוֹר הַחַיִּים bitzror hachayim,
וּתְהִי מְנוּחָתוֹ כָּבוֹד, ut·hi m'nuchato chavod,
שֹׂבַע שְׂמָחוֹת אֶת פָּנֶיךָ, sova smachot et panecha,
נְעִמוֹת בִּימִינְךָ נֶצַח. n'imot bimin'cha netzach.
וְנֹאמַר: אָמֵן. V'nomar: Amen.

May God remember the soul of my beloved son,
who has gone to his eternal reward.
May his soul be bound in the bonds of eternal life.
May he rest in the perfect joy of Your presence. Amen.

In memory of a daughter:

יִזְכּוֹר אֱלֹהִים	Yizkor Elohim
נִשְׁמַת בִּתִּי הָאֲהוּבָה...	nishmat biti ha·ahuvah…
מַחְמַד עֵינַי שֶׁהָלְכָה לְעוֹלָמָהּ.	machmad einai shehal'cha l'olamah.
אָנָּא תִּהְיֶינָה נַפְשָׁהּ צְרוּרָה	Ana t'hiyenah nafshah tz'rurah
בִּצְרוֹר הַחַיִּים,	bitzror hachayim,
וּתְהִי מְנוּחָתָהּ כָּבוֹד,	ut·hi m'nuchatah kavod,
שֹׂבַע שְׂמָחוֹת אֶת פָּנֶיךָ,	sova s'machot et panecha,
נְעִמוֹת בִּימִינְךָ נֶצַח.	n'imot bimin'cha netzach.
וְנֹאמַר: אָמֵן.	V'nomar: Amen.

May God remember the soul of my beloved daughter
who has gone to her eternal reward.
May her soul be bound in the bonds of eternal life.
May she rest in the perfect joy of Your presence.

In memory of other relatives and friends:

יִזְכּוֹר אֱלֹהִים נִשְׁמוֹת קְרוֹבַי וְרֵעַי	Yizkor Elohim nishmot k'rovai v'rei·ai
שֶׁהָלְכוּ לְעוֹלָמָם,	she'halchu l'olamam,
שֶׁבְּלִי נֶדֶר אֶתֵּן צְדָקָה בְּעַד	shebli neder etein tz'dakah ba·ad
הַזְכָּרַת נִשְׁמוֹתֵיהֶם.	hazkarat nishmoteihem.
אָנָּא תִּהְיֶינָה נַפְשׁוֹתֵיהֶם צְרוּרוֹת	Ana tihyenah nafshoteihem tz'rurot
בִּצְרוֹר הַחַיִּים, וּתְהִי מְנוּחָתָם כָּבוֹד,	bitzror hachayim ut·hi m'nuchatam kavod,
שֹׂבַע שְׂמָחוֹת אֶת פָּנֶיךָ,	sova smachot et-panecha,
נְעִמוֹת בִּימִינְךָ נֶצַח.	n'imot bimin'cha netzach.
וְנֹאמַר: אָמֵן.	V'nomar: Amen.

May God remember the soul of my relatives and friends
who have gone to their eternal reward.
I pledge acts of justice and charity in their memories.
May their souls be bound in the bonds of eternal life.
May they rest in the perfect joy of Your presence. Amen.

In memory of those who died to sanctify God's Name:

יִזְכּוֹר אֱלֹהִים נִשְׁמוֹת   Yizkor Elohim nishmot
כָּל־אַחֵֽינוּ וְכָל־אַחוֹתֵֽינוּ,   kol-acheinu v'kol-achoteinu,
בְּנֵי יִשְׂרָאֵל שֶׁמָּסְרוּ אֶת־נַפְשָׁם   b'nei Yisra·el shemasru et-nafsham
עַל קִדּוּשׁ הַשֵּׁם.   al kidush Hasheim.
שֶׁבְּלִי נֶֽדֶר אֶתֵּן צְדָקָה בְּעַד   Shebli neder etein tz'dakah ba·ad
הַזְכָּרַת נִשְׁמוֹתֵיהֶם.   hazkarat nishmoteihem.
אָנָּא יִשָּׁמַע בְּחַיֵּֽינוּ הֵד גְּבוּרָתָם   Ana yishama b'chayeinu heid g'vuratam
וּמְסִירוּתָם, וְיֵרָאֶה בְּמַעֲשֵֽׂינוּ   um'sirutam v'yareih b'maaseinu
טֹהַר לִבָּם,   tohar libam,
וְתִהְיֶֽינָה נַפְשׁוֹתֵיהֶם צְרוּרוֹת   v'tihyenah nafshoteihem tz·rurot
בִּצְרוֹר הַחַיִּים וּתְהִי מְנוּחָתָם כָּבוֹד,   bitzror hachayim ut·hi m'nuchatam kavod,
שֹֽׂבַע שְׂמָחוֹת אֶת פָּנֶֽיךָ,   sova s'machot et panecha,
נְעִמוֹת בִּימִינְךָ נֶֽצַח.   n'imot bimin'cha netzach.
וְנֹאמַר: אָמֵן.   V'nomar: Amen.

May God remember the souls of our brothers and sisters,
martyrs of our people, who gave their lives for the sanctification of God's name.
I pledge acts of justice and charity in their memories.
May echoes of their bravery and devotion be heard in our lives
and may the purity of their hearts be seen in our actions.
May their souls be bound in the bonds of eternal life.
May they rest in the perfect joy of Your presence. Amen.

El Malei Rachamim

This Yizkor El Maleh is written in the plural, speaking of "the souls" of those who have died. Other iterations of El Maleh in this book are written in the singular, referencing a single soul; the same is true of Elah M'leiat Rachamim which accompanies El Maleh everywhere it appears in this book.

אֵל מָלֵא רַחֲמִים,   El Malei rachamim,

שׁוֹכֵן בַּמְּרוֹמִים,   shochein bamromim.

הַמְצֵא מְנוּחָה נְכוֹנָה   Hamtzei m'nuchah n'chonah

תַּחַת כַּנְפֵי הַשְּׁכִינָה,   tachat kanfei haShechinah,

עִם קְדוֹשִׁים וּטְהוֹרִים   im k'doshim ut'horim

כְּזֹהַר הָרָקִיעַ מַזְהִירִים   k'zohar haraki·a maz·hirim

אֶת נִשְׁמוֹת יַקִּירֵינוּ   et nishmot yakireinu

שֶׁהָלְכוּ לְעוֹלָמָם,   shehal'chu l'olamam,

בְּגַן עֵדֶן תְּהֵא מְנוּחָתָם.   b'Gan Eden t'hei m'nuchatam.

לָכֵן בַּעַל הָרַחֲמִים יַסְתִּירֵם   Lachein ba·al harachamim yastirem

בְּסֵתֶר כְּנָפָיו לְעוֹלָמִים,   b'seiter k'nafav l'olamim,

וְיִצְרוֹר בִּצְרוֹר הַחַיִּים   v'yitzror bitzror hachayim

אֶת נִשְׁמוֹתֵיהֶם,   et-nishmoteihem,

יהוה הוּא נַחֲלָתָם.   Adonai Hu nachalatam.

וְיָנוּחוּ בְשָׁלוֹם עַל מִשְׁכְּבוֹתֵיהֶם.   V'yanuchu b'shalom al mishk'voteiheim.

וְנֹאמַר: אָמֵן.   V'nomar: Amen.

Compassionate God, Spirit of the universe,
grant perfect peace
in Your sheltering Presence,
among the holy and the pure,
who shine with the splendor
of the heavens,
to the souls of our dear ones
who have gone to their reward,
may the Garden of Eden
be their rest. O God of mercy,
guard them forever in the shadow of Your wings.
May their souls be bound up
in the bond of life.
May they rest in peace.
And let us say: Amen.

Elah M'lei·at Rachamim

This version of El Malei Rachamim uses feminine Hebrew,
speaking to divinity in feminine form.

אֵלָה מְלֵאַת רַחֲמִים   Elah m'lei·at rachamim,

שׁוֹכֶנֶת בַּמְּרוֹמִים,   shochenet bam'romim,

הַמְצִיאִי מְנוּחָה נְכוֹנָה   hamtzi·i m'nuchah n'chonah

תַּחַת כַּנְפֵי הַשְּׁכִינָה   tachat kanfei hashechinah

בְּמַעֲלוֹת קְדוֹשׁוֹת וּטְהוֹרוֹת   b'ma·alot k'doshot ut·horot

כְּזֹהַר הָרָקִיעַ מַזְהִירוֹת   k'zohar haraki·a maz·hirot

אֶת נִשְׁמַת _____   et nishmat _____

שֶׁהָלְכָה לְעוֹלָמָהּ   shehal'chah l'olamah

בְּגַן עֵדֶן תְּהֵא מְנוּחָתָהּ.   b'Gan Eden t'hei m'nuchatah.

אָנָּא גְּבִירַת הָרַחֲמִים   Ana g'virat harachamim

תַּסְתִּירִיהָ בְּצֵל כְּנָפַיִךְ   tastirihah betzel k'nafayich

לְעוֹלָמִים, וְצִרְרִי בִּצְרוֹר הַחַיִּים   l'olamim, v'tzir'ri bitzror hachayim

אֶת נִשְׁמָתָהּ,   et nishmatah,

שְׁכִינָה הִיא נַחֲלָתָהּ.   Shechinah hi nachalatah.

וְתָנוּחַ בְּשָׁלוֹם עַל מִשְׁכָּבָהּ.   V'tanu·ach b'shalom al mishkavah.

וְנֹאמַר: אָמֵן.   V'nomar: Amen.

God filled with mercy,
dwelling in the heavens' heights,
bring proper rest
beneath the wings of Your Shechinah,
amid the ranks of the holy and the pure
shining like the brilliance of the skies,
to the soul of our beloved _____
who has gone to her eternal place of rest.
May her rest be in the Garden of Eden.
May You who are the source of mercy
shelter her beneath Your wings eternally,
and weave her soul into the web of life
that she may rest in peace.
And let us say: Amen.

(Rabbi Jill Hammer)

Psalm 23

מִזְמוֹר לְדָוִד,
Mizmor l'David.

יהוה רֹעִי, לֹא אֶחְסָר.
יהוה ro·i, lo echsar.

בִּנְאוֹת דֶּשֶׁא יַרְבִּיצֵנִי,
Binot desheh yarbitzeini,

עַל מֵי מְנֻחוֹת יְנַהֲלֵנִי.
al mei menuchot y'nahaleini.

נַפְשִׁי יְשׁוֹבֵב,
Nafshi y'shoveiv,

יַנְחֵנִי בְמַעְגְּלֵי צֶדֶק,
yancheini v'mag'lei tzedek,

לְמַעַן שְׁמוֹ.
lema·an sh'mo.

גַּם כִּי אֵלֵךְ בְּגֵיא צַלְמָוֶת,
Gam ki eilech b'gei tzalmavet,

לֹא אִירָא רָע כִּי אַתָּה עִמָּדִי,
lo ira ra, ki atah imadi,

שִׁבְטְךָ וּמִשְׁעַנְתֶּךָ,
shivt'cha umishantecha,

הֵמָּה יְנַחֲמֻנִי.
heimah y'nachamuni.

תַּעֲרֹךְ לְפָנַי, שֻׁלְחָן נֶגֶד צֹרְרָי,
Ta·aroch lefanai, shulchan neged tzor'rai,

דִּשַּׁנְתָּ בַשֶּׁמֶן רֹאשִׁי,
dishanta vashemen roshi

כּוֹסִי רְוָיָה.
kosi r'vayah.

אַךְ טוֹב וָחֶסֶד יִרְדְּפוּנִי
Ach tov vachesed yird'funi

כָּל יְמֵי חַיָּי,
kol y'mei chayai,

וְשַׁבְתִּי בְּבֵית יהוה
v'shavti b'veit יהוה

לְאֹרֶךְ יָמִים.
l'orech yamim.

A psalm of David:

יהוה is my shepherd; I shall not want.
God makes me lie down in green pastures
and leads me beside still waters to restore my soul;
God leads me in paths of righteousness
for the sake of God's name.
Though I walk through the valley
of the shadow of death,
I shall fear no evil,
for You are with me;
Your rod and Your staff,
they comfort me.
You set a table before me
in the presence of my enemies.
You anoint my head with oil;
my cup overflows.
Truly goodness and mercy
will follow me
all the days of my life,
and I will dwell
in the house of יהוה forever.

The Valley of Shadow

גַּם כִּי אֵלֵךְ בְּגֵיא צַלְמָוֶת   Gam ki elech b'gei tzalmavet
לֹא אִירָא רָע.   lo ira ra.

"Yea, though I walk through the Valley of the Shadow of Death, I will fear no evil," says the psalm. I used to think this passage was about the fear of death: anticipation of it. When I'm afraid for my life, God is with me. That's what I was sure the psalmist was aiming for.

But now I'm no longer certain. Because it is now — after my mother's death, not in anticipation of it — that I am walking in *gei tzalmavet*. Death casts a shadow that obscures the road ahead. It is not an evil road that I'm on! Just a shadowed one. Out of focus, making makes routine things seem out of place.

But there's another piece I'm feeling about this road. The Hebrew *tzalmavet*, "shadow of death," could also be read as *tzalmut* — meaning something like "self-image" or "identity," from the root *tzelem* that we use when we say we are made in God's image.

Walking the path, after losing parents, is a challenge of *tzalmut*, of identity. Who am I now? What does it mean for me to be me, now that none of being me can be about pleasing my mother— or rebelling against her? Who am I now that I can't see myself reflected in her eyes? Who am I now that I am on the front edge of the generations? Who will I become? How will I change? When I look at my reflection in the mirror, will I see more of her now, or less?

גַּם כִּי אֵלֵךְ בְּגֵיא צַלְמָוֶת   Gam ki elech b'gey tzalmavet
לֹא אִירָא רָע.   lo ira ra.

But as I walk through the valley of this precarious new identity, I will not fear. Because it is not an evil road. Just a shadowed one, hard to see around the next bend.

When people ask, "How are you," I've begun to simply say, "The jury's out." I'm sad, I'm bewildered, I'm busy, and I'm wondering who I am. But: *lo ira ra*. I'm not afraid.

(Irwin Keller)

Mourner's Kaddish

יִתְגַּדַּל וְיִתְקַדַּשׁ שְׁמֵהּ רַבָּא,
Yitgadal v'yitkadash, sh'meih raba,

בְּעָלְמָא דִּי בְרָא כִרְעוּתֵהּ,
b'al'ma di v'ra chiruteih,

וְיַמְלִיךְ מַלְכוּתֵהּ
v'yamlich malchuteih

בְּחַיֵּיכוֹן וּבְיוֹמֵיכוֹן
b'chayeichon uvyomeichon

וּבְחַיֵּי דְּכָל בֵּית יִשְׂרָאֵל,
uvchayei d'chol beit Yisra·el,

בַּעֲגָלָא וּבִזְמַן קָרִיב,
ba·agala uvizman kariv,

וְאִמְרוּ: אָמֵן.
v'imru: **Amen.**

יְהֵא שְׁמֵהּ רַבָּא מְבָרַךְ
Y'hei sh'mei raba m'varach

לְעָלַם וּלְעָלְמֵי עָלְמַיָּא.
l'alam ulal'mei al'maya.

יִתְבָּרַךְ וְיִשְׁתַּבַּח, וְיִתְפָּאַר
Yitbarach v'yishtabach v'yitpa·ar

וְיִתְרוֹמַם וְיִתְנַשֵּׂא וְיִתְהַדָּר וְיִתְעַלֶּה
v'yit·romam v'yitnasei v'yit·hadar v'yitaleh

וְיִתְהַלָּל שְׁמֵהּ דְּקֻדְשָׁא
v'yit·halal sh'meih d'kudsha

בְּרִיךְ הוּא
b'rich hu

לְעֵלָּא
l'eila

During the Ten Days of Repentance:

וּלְעֵלָּא
uleila

מִן כָּל בִּרְכָתָא וְשִׁירָתָא,
min kol birchata v'shirata,

תֻּשְׁבְּחָתָא וְנֶחֱמָתָא,
tushb'chata v'nechemata,

דַּאֲמִירָן בְּעָלְמָא, וְאִמְרוּ: **אָמֵן.**
da·amiran b'al'ma, v'imru: Amen.

יְהֵא שְׁלָמָא רַבָּא מִן שְׁמַיָּא
Y'hei sh'lama raba min sh'maya

וְחַיִּים עָלֵינוּ וְעַל כָּל יִשְׂרָאֵל,
v'chayim aleinu v'al kol Yisra·el,

וְאִמְרוּ: אָמֵן.
v'imru: Amen.

עֹשֶׂה שָׁלוֹם בִּמְרוֹמָיו
Oseh shalom bimromav,

הוּא יַעֲשֶׂה שָׁלוֹם עָלֵינוּ
hu ya·aseh shalom, aleinu

וְעַל כָּל יִשְׂרָאֵל,
v'al kol Yisra·el,

וְעַל כָּל יוֹשְׁבֵי תֵבֵל,
v'al kol yosh'vei teiveil,

וְאִמְרוּ: **אָמֵן.**
v'imru: **Amen.**

Secular-Friendly Kaddish Translation

There is an eternal essence that persists in time and space —
and this is our prayer to make it part of our awareness
by affirming its persistence and pledging ourselves
to act to advance the promise it holds of a better world;
may it be soon and in our days. Amen.

Let the great essence be blessed through all our actions!

Whether it be blessed or praised or honored or exalted,
we affirm that it is far beyond any expression which we use to describe it —
prayer or song, prose or poem — and we say: Amen

We express our hopes for peace and for life upon us and upon all people. Amen.

May the harmony we experience as we gaze toward heaven
be reflected in a harmony between all who dwell on the planet:
Israelite, Ishmaelite, and all creatures upon this holy earth, and we say: Amen.

(translation: Rabbi David Cooper)

(Each time Mourner's Kaddish appears in this volume,
it is translated by someone different. Each translation is unique,
and each evokes a particular quality of the original Aramaic.)

Mourner's Kaddish for Every Day

Build me up of memory
loving and angry, tender and honest.
Let my loss build me a heart of wisdom,
compassion for the world's many losses

Each hour is mortal
and each hour is eternal
and each hour is our testament.
May I create worthy memories
all the days of my life

(Debra Cash)

Psalm 130

From the deepest place within me, I call out to You.
God, hear what is in my voice.
Hear my pleading tone.
Were You to look for imperfection—
who could stand it? Who could stand it?
You are so generous with pardon, but we fear to seek it.
Still I hope, God. My very soul hopes for it:
Please send me Your loving word.
Among the watchers for the dawn, my God,
I yearn for Your grace to end my darkness.
Israel looks to You, God, who are so gracious.
So easily You can free all of us.
Lift us from all our brokenness.

(adapted from Rabbi Zalman Schachter-Shalomi z"l)

Other Prayers

Candles (For a Stillbirth)

And there you are in my arms
in a dress with ruffles grinning with just two teeth
as everyone sings to you,
and that's you with handfuls of wrapping paper,
your face smeared with frosting,
and look at you there, showing your doll
how to cut the cake,
and it seems impossible that it's been four years
of me lighting candles you'll never see,
flickering dimly in their fireproof glass,
on the day you were born too soon,
on the day you should have been born,
on the day of remembering
all the birthdays I wanted you to have.

(Nancie Martin)

Request (After a Miscarriage)

Source of all that is
source of mercy
planter of seeds
in rocky soil

You whose names
are womb
and breast
and giver of milk

protect everyone
who aims imperfectly
to emulate
your loving care

guard everyone
who opens her body
and prays
for possibility

grant us compassion
when our bodies fail us
and help us try
again, and again

remind us
that deep down
something new waits
always to grow.

(Rabbi Rachel Barenblat)

The Longest Night (For Parents of a Child Who Has Died)

We all tell ourselves stories
about grief to come.

Anticipating the dark
we think, how can I live

without the sun I turn toward?
We wrest what gifts we can

from the dying days.
One morning we wake

and the doorway we most dreaded
is behind us.

The ice may not recede
for months to come

but day by day
may there be more light.

(Rabbi Rachel Barenblat)
for Phyllis and Michael Sommer

The Grave Not Opened

Seeing a round stone as I walk a muddy trail,
I kneel to dislodge it from the soil where it lies.
Reaching fingers raise the rock above my head,
Placing mineral as marker in the vital skies.

I long for a memorial to set the stone upon.
Your face and name are etched only in my mind.
No place to idle my always-aching gaze,
Your body rests nowhere that I can find.

I pray my love for you will never crumble.
Round stones remind me, wherever they may be:
Time shaves off our edges, leaving smooth relics —
My wish that you were still here with me.

(Rabbi Evan Krame)

What Is a Grave For?

A place for telling stories
A place for communing
With...

A place to be with...
Or perhaps to be with
Someone else?

But what if we
Could make that place
Of ourselves?

Imagine how to do that
How much freer it might
Feel to know that

You could reach out,
Wherever you are,
And touch the core

Of the one who
Has no grave
To visit.

(Rabbi Cynthia Hoffman)

When There Is No Grave To Visit

We scatter your ashes at sea,
riding far into the waters in a speeding boat,
strewing your remains onto the choppy waves.
I pray: May God bless you and protect you.
The boat turns and we race to land and home.
I look back and cannot see you.

I turn this way and that, not knowing where to face,
not knowing where you are,
knowing you are not here.
I pray: May God's light shine on you and be gracious to you.
I turn again, pray in another direction,
turn again and again.

I stand at the edge of the sea,
cold curls of water dance up to my feet
and coyly slip away. You are not here.
I pray: May God's face be lifted toward you,
and toward me,
and bestow upon us peace.

(Rabbi Jennifer Singer)

When The Grave Is Too Far Away

God, my loved one is buried
Too far away to visit.
I want to run my fingers along
Their name, engraved in granite.
To take a stone from my pocket
And leave it to mark my presence.

Times like this, I wish
I didn't live so far away.
If I close my eyes and imagine
Their headstone here before me
Will You help me feel as though
I'd actually gone to see them?

Be the switchboard operator:
Please connect my call.
When I say "I remember you"
I want to believe they hear me
Even though I'm not standing
In that far-off cemetery.

May the miles between here
And there become unimportant
In the face of what connects us
Across every kind of distance.

(Rabbi Rachel Barenblat)

In Remembrance of an Abusive Relationship

1.

I mourn the self
Who was Hurt deeply
Profoundly
Painfully
Who was lost for a time in the noise
of someone else's story
Their need to
Control
Destroy
Patch their own wounds
by making them mine

I was told in word and deed
That I was too much
Too smart
Too pretty
Too headstrong
Too damaged

I had yearnings and hopes
And they were dashed

I offered myself
And was rejected

My losses are found
In the marrow of my bones

When I weep
There is little comfort

2.

And yet –

May I dare to imagine
The life I may still live

May I remember that
I am not what they said
I am not what they did

May I know that while
I am weighted by memory
I am not my past

I am
Intrinsically
Beautifully
More than they believed

I am a vessel for thoughts
And words
And song
And patience
And love
And compassion
And stillness
That without me would not be born
Into a world that needs these things
Like breath

3.

I claim resilience for myself
For the others who've walked
This path before me

I remember that for those who follow
I am hope

I exist in this moment
And for myself
I am love

(Cate Denial)

Prayer for Those Left Behind After the Suicide of a Loved One

May the One who blessed our ancestors, Abraham, Isaac, Jacob, Sarah, Rebecca, Rachel and Leah and all those who came after them, bless those of us living in the shadow of the valley of death, left behind because of the suffering of a dear soul who took their own life.

May our connection with the One who is the Source of All Blessing, continually remind us that our memories of our loved ones are for a blessing: *zichronam livracha*. May we be able to look at their life and not only their suffering and death. May we learn to understand in time that memories of their life bless our days. May we know through our memories of their life, they too, are blessed wherever they rest. May they be protected by the God of Compassion.

When the memories of their life's suffering come to us, give us the strength and courage to feel compassion and love for them. Help us feel the companionship of families, friends, ancestors, and the Divine Presence to protect and nourish us in times of distress. May we find the healing possible through sharing our whole experience with others, including feelings of regret and shame, relief and anger, grief and sorrow, unanswered questions, and deep love.

Source of All Life, surround us with grace and spread over us a sukkat shalom, a shelter of peace and wholeness. And let us say Amen.

(Rabbi Chaya Gusfield)

A Yizkor Kavanah for the Ambivalent

Bless Yah, Ruach Ha Olam,
Breathing us in and breathing us out.
Each loss breaks a pattern.
We pray and remember.

Daddy God of our childhood.
Useless God of our arrogant youth,
Intervening God of our adult actions,
Mother God of our spiritual seeking,
Soothing God of our old age,
Listening God of our last words,
We pray and remember.

Bless Yah, Ruach Ha Olam,
Breathing us in and breathing us out.
Imagining us,
Comforting us,
Singing us,
We pray and remember.

We remember them:
Our Teachers and Leaders,
Our Artists and Entertainers,
Our Enemies and Rivals,
Our Friends and Companions,
Our Aunts and Uncles and Cousins,
Our Husbands and Wives and Partners,
Our Children and Siblings,
Our Parents and Grandparents.

We remember them
Because we loved each other,
Except when we didn't.

We pray and we hope for delight in the memories
And music when there cannot be joy
And repair when the patterns break.

Bless Yah, breathing in,
Praying with us because we are alone.
Bless Yah, breathing out,
Remembering us when we cannot.

(Trisha Arlin)

Prayers for comfort

When You Cry Out

You think I'm not listening.
You can't feel my hand
on your shoulderblade, my lips

pressed to your forehead
my heart, ground down with yours
into the dust of the earth.

Sweet one, I feel your grief
like a black hole inside my chest
strong enough to swallow galaxies.

I can't lift it from you.
All I can do is cry with you
until I struggle for breath

all I can do is love you
with a force as limitless as gravity,
endless as the uncountable stars.

(Rabbi Rachel Barenblat)

Low Bench

I return to the low bench.
Kaddish on the bright cusp of solace
year after illumined year

(Maxine Silverman)

If Only

Oseh shalom bimromav
O God, I could bear the loss
If only I did not have to remember
And I could bear the memories
If only they did not bring such pain,
And I could bear the pain
If only I could weep,
And weeping, water
The seedlings of care.

Hu ya·aseh shalom
Blessed are You, Great Heart,
Who grows sprouts of love
Amidst freshly dug roots.

(Rabbi Shohama Harris Wiener)

Missing You

Dear one, I left love notes
for you everywhere today —

tucked into the petals
of the tulip magnolia

encoded in the braille
of black willow bark,

hidden in the patterns of rain
on your windshield

— but you didn't notice.
My missives remain unread.

Your despair renders me
invisible. You forget

I'm right here. How
can I balm your sorrows?

If only you could hear me
in the ring of your phone.

Feel my fingers
twined with yours, my kiss

on the tender place
in the middle of your palm.

(Rabbi Rachel Barenblat)

Broken-Hearted (HaRofei, Psalm 147)

הָרֹפֵא לִשְׁבוּרֵי לֵב   Harofei lishvurei lev
וּמְחַבֵּשׁ לְעַצְּבוֹתָם.   umchabeish l'atz'votam.

מוֹנֶה מִסְפָּר לַכּוֹכָבִים   Moneh mispar lakochavim
לְכֻלָּם שֵׁמוֹת יִקְרָא.   l'chulam sheimot yikra.

> Healer of the broken-hearted
> Binder of their wounds
> Counter of uncountable stars
> You know where they are.
>
> Healer of the broken-hearted
> Binder of our wounds
> Counter of uncountable stars
> You know who we are.

הַלְלוּ יָהּ.   Hal'lu-Yah. x2
אָנָא, אֵל נָא,   Ana, El na,
רְפָא נָא לָהּ.   R'fa na lah.

אָנָא אֵל נָא.   Ana, El na,
רְפָא נָא לָהּ.   R'fa na lah. x2
הַלְלוּ יָהּ.   Hal'lu-Yah. x2

(Shir Yaakov Feit)
(Listen at shiryaakov.bandcamp.com/track/broken-hearted-harofei-psalm-147)

We Are a Spiral (Ki Afar At)

כִּי עָפָר אָתְּ,   Ki afar at,
וְאֶל עָפָר תָּשׁוּבִי.   v'el afar tashuvi.

> Earth we are and earth we will be
> We are a spiral coming home

(Kohenet Taya Shere)
(Listen at holytaya.bandcamp.com/track/we-are-a-spiral)

Remembrance

To Every Thing There Is A Season

Ecclesiastes 3:1-8

To every thing there is a season,
and a time to every purpose under heaven.
A time to be born, and a time to die,
A time to plant, and a time to uproot.
A time to kill, and a time to heal,
A time to break down, and a time to build up.
A time to weep, and a time to laugh,
A time to mourn, and a time to dance.
A time to cast away stones, and a time to gather them together,
A time to embrace, and a time to refrain from embracing.
A time to seek, and a time to lose,
A time to keep, and a time to cast away.
A time to rend, and a time to sew,
A time to keep silence, and a time to speak.

We Enter The World...

Ecclesiastes Rabbah 5:14

We enter the world in the same way we depart.
We enter with a cry and go with a cry.
We enter with weeping and go with weeping.
We enter with love and go with love.
We enter with a sigh and go with a sigh.
We enter without knowing and go without knowing.
It has been taught in the name of Rabbi Meir:
When we enter the world our hands are clenched, as if to say,
"The whole world is mine. I shall inherit it."
But when we take leave of it, our hands are spread open,
as if to say, "I have taken nothing from the world."

Life is Born (Dor Holeich)

Based on Ecclesiastes 1:1, 4-7, inspired by Nelly Sachs.

דּוֹר הֹלֵךְ וְדוֹר בָּא,	Dor holeich v'dor ba,
וְהָאָרֶץ לְעוֹלָם עֹמָדֶת.	v'ha·aretz l'olam omadet.
וְזָרַח הַשֶּׁמֶשׁ, וּבָא הַשָּׁמֶשׁ	V'zarach hashemesh, uva hashamesh
וְאֶל מְקוֹמוֹ שׁוֹאֵף זוֹרֵחַ	v'el m'komo sho·eif zorei·ach.
הוֹלֵךְ אֶל דָּרוֹם	Holeich el darom
וְסוֹבֵב אֶל צָפוֹן סוֹבֵב סֹבֵב	v'soveiv el tzafon soveiv soveiv
הוֹלֵךְ הָרוּחַ.	holeich haruach.
כָּל הַנְּחָלִים הוֹלְכִים אֶל הַיָּם,	Kol han'chalim hol'chim el hayam
וְהַיָּם אֵינֶנּוּ מָלֵא.	vehayam einenu malei.
כָּךְ הַתְחָלָה זוֹרֶמֶת	Kach hatchalah zoremet
אֶל סוֹף קֵץ זוֹרֵם אֶל רֵאשִׁית	el sof keitz zoreim el reishit
הָאַחֲרוֹנָה הִיא הָרִאשׁוֹנָה.	ha·acharonah hi harishonah.
הֲבֵל הֲבָלִים הֲבֵל הַכֹּל.	Haveil havalim haveil hakol.

Life is born and life moves on and the earth has held and will hold it all.
The sun rises and the sun sets and returns again to rise and fall.
The wind turns south and the wind turns north,
turning, turning, returning still.
The rivers run from the clouds to the sea
and become the rain, and the sea is never filled.
So the beginning moves to the end and the end flows on to begin again.
The one at the end is the one who begins and
the breath of breaths is within all things.

(Rabbi Jill Hammer)

Longing, exit 16

Turn here
if your heart aches

if someone you love
is out of reach

if a beloved
is suffering

and you wish
more than anything—

Turn here
if you've wanted

what you didn't have
or couldn't have

if love overflows
like an open faucet

if yearning is as close
as you get to whole.

(Rabbi Rachel Barenblat)

God Who Illumines

God who illumines our days by sun,
our nights by moon,
illuminate the path of _____
by the light of your face
as their days are ended.

God who brought us forth from the womb
and who gives us a finite time
to walk this this earth: we know
we have no control over our birth
and we cannot escape our death.

God who accompanies us
as we gather in memory,
who accompanies each soul's journey
strengthen us to bring comfort
to all who mourn.

(Rabbi Evan Krame)

Night Light

After we buried our father, the moon came nearest
earth's center, resplendent in its wholeness,
most expansive night of all other nights,
the Shiva Moon.

Every full moon since, I report the news
as if visiting his far away grave, my night words
the stones laid on his stone, homely words, rough,
unburnished, steadfast. I say how I miss him still,
how his grandsons grew, how they fare.
If no one else is walking her dog, I might sing.

(Maxine Silverman)

Birdwings

Your grief for what you've lost lifts a mirror
up to where you're bravely working.

Expecting the worst, you look, and instead,
here's the joyful face you've been wanting to see.

Your hand opens and closes and opens and closes.
If it were always a fist or always stretched open,
you would be paralyzed.

Your deepest presence
is in every small contracting and expanding,
the two as beautifully balanced and coordinated
as birdwings.

(Rumi, translated by Coleman Barks)

Not all women

"Not all women, trees, or ovens are identical." — Mishnah Pesachim 3:4, in the name of R' Akiva

Some women like winter. Some incubate babies
and some have no uterus. Some wear eyeliner.

Some are happiest in Israeli sandals
flaunting our pedicured toes.

Some are stronger than the steel cables
that hold up a suspension bridge.

Some are notorious.
Some write love poems.

Some have roots that go deep
into the earth and will not be shaken.

Some give our fruit and branches
and trunk until we are nothing but stumps.

Some grow thorns to protect ourselves
even if we're vilified for it.

Some women are more like trees
than like ovens: constantly changing.

Some women are nourishing and warm.
Some women burn with holy fire.

Some are irreducible, incomparable
like the Holy One of Blessing Herself.

Some women balance justice and mercy.
Some are mirrors: we'll give kindness

as we receive, but injustice causes
our eyes to blaze the world into ash.

(Rabbi Rachel Barenblat)

Every Person Has a Name

Every person has a name given by God given by her parents.	לְכָל אִישׁ יֵשׁ שֵׁם שֶׁנָּתַן לוֹ אֱלֹהִים וְנָתְנוּ לוֹ אָבִיו וְאִמּוֹ.	L'chol ish yesh sheim shenatan lo Elohim v'nat'nu lo aviv v'imo.
Every person has a name given by his appearance given by her clothes.	לְכָל אִישׁ יֵשׁ שֵׁם שֶׁנָּתְנוּ לוֹ קוֹמָתוֹ וְאֹפֶן חִיּוּכוֹ וְנָתַן לוֹ הָאָרִיג.	L'chol ish yesh sheim shenat'nu lo komato v'ofen chiyucho v'natan lo ha·arig.
Every person has a name given by the mountains and given by his walls.	לְכָל אִישׁ יֵשׁ שֵׁם שֶׁנָּתְנוּ לוֹ הֶהָרִים וְנָתְנוּ לוֹ כְּתָלָיו.	L'chol ish yesh sheim shenat'nu lo heharim v'nat'nu lo k'talav.
Every person has a name given by the stars given by her neighbors.	לְכָל אִישׁ יֵשׁ שֵׁם שֶׁנָּתְנוּ לוֹ הַמַּזָּלוֹת וְנָתְנוּ לוֹ שְׁכֵנָיו.	L'chol ish yesh sheim shenat'nu lo hamazalot v'nat'nu lo sh'cheinav.
Every person has a name given by his sins given by her yearning.	לְכָל אִישׁ יֵשׁ שֵׁם שֶׁנָּתְנוּ לוֹ חֲטָאָיו וְנָתְנָה לוֹ כְּמִיהָתוֹ.	L'chol ish yesh sheim shenat'nu lo chatav v'nat"nu lo k'mihato.
Every person has a name given by his enemies, given by her love.	לְכָל אִישׁ יֵשׁ שֵׁם שֶׁנָּתְנוּ לוֹ שׂוֹנְאָיו וְנָתְנָה לוֹ אַהֲבָתוֹ.	L'chol ish yesh sheim shenat'nu lo sonav v'nat'na lo ahavato.
Every person has a name given by his holidays, given by her toil.	לְכָל אִישׁ יֵשׁ שֵׁם שֶׁנָּתְנוּ לוֹ חַגָּיו וְנָתְנָה לוֹ מְלַאכְתּוֹ.	L'chol ish yesh sheim shenat'nu lo chagiv v'nat'na lo m'lachto.
Every person has a name given by the seasons, given by his blindness.	לְכָל אִישׁ יֵשׁ שֵׁם שֶׁנָּתְנוּ לוֹ תְּקוּפוֹת הַשָּׁנָה וְנָתַן לוֹ עִוְרוֹנוֹ.	L'chol ish yesh sheim shenat'nu lo t'kufot hashanah v'natan lo ivrono.
Every person has a name given by the sea, given by her death.	לְכָל אִישׁ יֵשׁ שֵׁם שֶׁנָּתַן לוֹ הַיָּם וְנָתַן לוֹ מוֹתוֹ.	L'chol ish yesh sheim shenatan lo hayam v'natan lo moto.

(Zelda Schneersohn Mishkovsky)

Songs from Psalms

Shiviti יהוה L'negdi Tamid (Psalm 16:8)

שִׁוִּיתִי יהוה לְנֶגְדִּי תָּמִיד. Shiviti יהוה l'negdi tamid.
I keep יהוה before me always.

Lach Amar Libi (Psalm 27:8)

לְךָ	Lach
אָמַר לִבִּי	amar libi
בַּקְּשׁוּ פָנָי	bak'shu fanai
בַּקְּשׁוּ פָנָי.	bak'shu fanai.
אֶת פָּנֶיךָ,	Et panayich,
הֲוָיָ"ה,	havayah,
אֲבַקֵּשׁ.	Avakeish.

You
Called to my heart:
Come seek My face,
Come seek My grace.
For Your love
Source of all
I will seek.

(translation: Rabbi David Markus)

Kavei el יהוה (Psalm 27:14)

קַוֵּה קַוֵּה	Kavei kavei,
קַוֵּה אֶל יהוה.	kavei el יהוה.
חֲזַק וְיַאֲמֵץ	chazak v'ya·ametz
לִבֶּךָ	libecha,
וְקַוֵּה אֶל יהוה.	v'kavei el יהוה.

Keep hope, keep hope
Keep hoping in the One
Be strong and open
Your heart wide
And keep hoping in the One!

(translation: Rabbi David Markus)

Esa Einai (Psalm 121:1-2)

אֶשָּׂא עֵינַי אֶל הֶהָרִים.   Esa einai el heharim.
מֵאַיִן יָבֹא עֶזְרִי?   Mei·ayin yavo ezri?
עֶזְרִי מֵעִם יהוה,   Ezri mei·im יהוה,
עֹשֵׂה שָׁמַיִם וָאָרֶץ.   Oseh shamayim va'aretz.

I lift my eyes up to the mountains:
From where comes my help?
My help is from
the Holy Blessed One
Creator of the heavens
and the earth.

Ana B'cho·ach

This prayer is a mystical meditation attributed to Rabbi Nechunya ben Hakanah of the second century. Some say it contains seven mystical Names of God, and others say the whole prayer is one long divine Name. The first verse asks God to untie our tangled places — a sentiment that may be especially heartfelt during times of mourning.

אָנָּא בְּכֹחַ	Ana b'cho·ach	Source of Mercy,
גְּדֻלַּת יְמִינְךָ	g'dulat y'min'cha	With loving strength
תַּתִּיר צְרוּרָה.	tatir tz'rurah.	Untie our tangles.
קַבֵּל רִנַּת	Kabeil rinat	Your chanting folk
עַמְּךָ שַׂגְּבֵנוּ	am'cha sag'veinu	Raise high, make pure,
טַהֲרֵנוּ נוֹרָא.	tahareinu nora.	Accept our song.
נָא גִבּוֹר	Na gibor	Like Your own eye
דּוֹרְשֵׁי יִחוּדְךָ	dor'shei yichud'cha	Lord keep us safe
כְּבָבַת שָׁמְרֵם.	k'vavat shomreim.	Who union seek with You.
בָּרְכֵם טַהֲרֵם	Bar'cheim tahareim	Cleanse and bless us
רַחֲמֵם צִדְקָתְךָ	rachameim tzidkatcha	Infuse us ever
תָּמִיד גָּמְלֵם.	tamid gomleim.	With loving care.
חֲסִין קָדוֹשׁ	Chasin kadosh	Gracious source
בְּרוֹב טוּבְךָ	b'rov tuv'cha	Of holy power!
נַהֵל עֲדָתֶךָ.	naheil adatecha.	Do guide Your folk.
יָחִיד גֵּאֶה	Yachid gei·eh	Sublime and holy One
לְעַמְּךָ פְּנֵה	l'am'cha p'neih	Do turn to us
זוֹכְרֵי קְדֻשָּׁתֶךָ.	zoch'rei k'dushatecha.	Of holy chant.
שַׁוְעָתֵנוּ קַבֵּל	Shavateinu kabeil	Receive our prayer,
וּשְׁמַע צַעֲקָתֵנוּ	ushma tza·akateinu	Do hear our cry,
יוֹדֵעַ תַּעֲלֻמוֹת.	yodei·a ta·alumot.	Who secrets knows.
בָּרוּךְ שֵׁם	Baruch sheim	Through time and space
כְּבוֹד מַלְכוּתוֹ	k'vod malchuto	Your glory shines,
לְעוֹלָם וָעֶד.	l'olam va·ed.	Majestic One.

(Singable English translation
by Rabbi Zalman Schachter-Shalomi z"l)

Eli, Eli

אֵלִי, אֵלִי שֶׁלֹּא יִגָּמֵר לְעוֹלָם   Eli, Eli shelo yigameir l'olam
הַחוֹל וְהַיָּם   Hachol v'hayam
רִשְׁרוּשׁ שֶׁל הַמַּיִם   Rishrush shel hamayim
בְּרַק הַשָּׁמַיִם, תְּפִלַּת הָאָדָם.   B'rak hashamayim, t'filat haadam.

My God, my God, I pray that these things never end:
the sand and the sea, the rush of the waters,
the crash of the heavens, the prayer of the heart.

(Hannah Szenes)

Without

I can't see you, can't touch you
can't breathe, because without you—

but I'm never without you. Even
when all I am is ache.

Especially then. Press my fingers
to the delicate bones of my wrist

and there you are, accompanying me
with every beat of my yearning heart.

(Rabbi Rachel Barenblat)

SOURCES

"Waters of Healing" (Wiener). Reprinted with permission.

"*Vidui* (for all the ways)" (Hammer). Reprinted with permission.

"*Vidui* for mourners of painful relationships" (Jordan) also appears (with slight variations) in *Jewish Relational Care*, ed. Jack Bloom (2006) and in the *CCAR Rabbi's Manual* (2015). Reprinted with permission.

"*Vidui* Before Sleep" (Schachter-Shalomi). Reprinted from *Tikkun* magazine.

"The Tearing" (Madden), Ritualwell. Reprinted with permission.

"A Prayer During Aninut" (Pessah). Reprinted with permission.

"For One Who Did Not Want Ritual Mourning" (Shine), from *Siddur Sha'ar Zahav*. Reprinted with permission.

"Aninut" (Barenblat), *Brilliant Coroners* (Laupe House Press, 2007). Reprinted with permission.

"How Dying Works" (Bozarth). Reprinted with permission.

"Lentil" (Kamenetz). Reprinted with permission.

"Renewed Ashrei" (Krame). Reprinted with permission.

Shiviti image by Ba'al HaCochav, from Open Siddur.

"My Constant Shepherd" (Cohen). Reprinted with permission.

"Elah M'lei·ah Rachamim" (Hammer). Reprinted with permission.

Ein Od Milvado calligraphy by soferet Julie Seltzer. Reprinted with permission.

"Mourner's Kaddish Translation" (Jacobson). Reprinted with permission.

"Magnified and Sanctified" (Maller). Reprinted with permission.

"As We Bless" (Rogow). Reprinted with permission.

"Bar'chu, Dear One" (Friedman), based on a Sufi chant. Reprinted with permission.

"Evening" (Barenblat) first appeared on the blog Velveteen Rabbi, 2017. Reprinted with permission.

"Unending Love" (Shapiro). Reprinted with permission.

"Journey" (Hammer) first appeared in *Siddur HaKohanot*. Reprinted with permission.

"Places Of Holiness, Places Of Peace" (Nazimova). Reprinted with permission.

"Mourner's Kaddish Poem" (bat Tzedek). Reprinted with permission.

"In Memory Of A Hurtful Parent" (Saks), reprinted from My Jewish Learning.

"Filled To Overflowing" (Rosen) first appeared on the blog Yedid Nefesh in 2013. Reprinted with permission.

"Prayer for Going Through Papers" (Keller). Reprinted with permission.

"When Will I be Myself Again?" (Eron). Reprinted with permission.

"Dinner Alone" (Armet). Reprinted with permission.

"Mourning to Dancing" (Spier). Reprinted with permission.

"Prayer Before the Final Kaddish" (Gusfield). Reprinted with permission.

"In Remembrance of an Abusive Relationship" (Denial). Reprinted with permission.

"B'al'ma DiVra" (Hammer). Reprinted with permission.

"Mourner's Prayer" (Silverman) first appeared in *Shiva Moon* (Ben Yehuda Press, 2017). Reprinted with permission.

"Cold Solace" (Kaufman) first appeared in *The Sun*. Reprinted with permission.

"Yahrzeit" (Kamenetz) first appeared in *The Missing Jew* (Time Being Books, 1992). Reprinted with author's permission.

"The Valley of Shadow" (Keller). Reprinted with permission.

"Secular Translation of the Mourner's Kaddish" (Cooper). Reprinted with permission.

"Mourner's Kaddish for Every Day" (Cash). Reprinted from Ritualwell.

"Candles (for Stillbirth)" (Martin), from West End Synagogue. Awaiting reprint permission.

"Request (after Miscarriage)" (Barenblat), originally printed in *Through*. Reprinted with permission.

"Prayer for those Left Behind" (Gusfield). Reprinted with permission.

"A Yizkor Kavanah for the Ambivalent" (Arlin) first appeared in *Place Yourself* (Dimus Parrhesia Press 2018). Reprinted with permission. © Trisha Arlin 2019, and shared with a Creative Commons Attribution (CC BY) 4.0 International license <https://creativecommons.org/licenses/by/4.0/>.

"Broken Open" (Michaelson) first appeared in *The Gate of Tears* (Ben Yehuda Press, 2015). Reprinted with permission.

"When You Cry Out" (Barenblat) first appeared on the blog Velveteen Rabbi, 2017. Reprinted with permission.

"Low Bench" (Silverman) first appeared in *Shiva Moon* (Ben Yehuda Press, 2017). Reprinted with permission.

"Missing You" (Barenblat) first appeared on the blog Velveteen Rabbi, 2017. Reprinted with permission.

"Broken-Hearted" (Feit) appears at ShirYaakov.com. Reprinted with permission.

"We are a Spiral" (Shere) first appeared in *Siddur HaKohanot*. Reprinted with permission.

"To Every Thing there is a Season" (Kohelet). Public domain.

"We Enter the World" (Kohelet Rabbah). Public domain.

"Life is Born (Dor Holeich)" (Hammer) first appeared in *Siddur HaKohanot*. Reprinted with permission.

"Longing, exit 16" (Barenblat), *Texts to the Holy* (Ben Yehuda Press, 2018). Reprinted with permission.

"Without" (Barenblat), *Texts to the Holy* (Ben Yehuda Press, 2018). Reprinted with permission.

"Night Light" (Silverman), *Shiva Moon* (Ben Yehuda Press, 2017). Reprinted with permission.

"Birdwings" (Rumi, transl. Barks), from *The Essential Rumi*.

"Not all Women" (Barenblat) first appeared on the blog Velveteen Rabbi, 2017. Reprinted with permission.

"Every Person Has a Name" (Zelda) is in the public domain.